The Broke
and
Beautiful
Life

346 3736

To Mom and Dad
For being the best examples of hard work
and generosity I've ever known.

CONTENTS

INTRODUCTION

I'm just going to say it... *I love money...* and I don't think there's anything wrong with that. I don't believe that money is the root of all evil. I don't think that it can buy happiness, either. But I do believe that it can provide *freedom*.

Financial freedom. What a glorious idea.

Not absurd wealth, just enough money to pay the rent, support yourself, support a family, and maybe take an occasional vacation or indulge in a day at the spa. The freedom to live without the stress of this month's bills or how you're going to put your children through college (or afford to have them in the first place). The freedom of *choosing* to work rather than *having* to work through retirement.

That's the dream. My dream, at least. And I'm set on getting there. But to be perfectly honest, I'm broke. I can barely support myself. Being a college graduate at the height of the financial crisis didn't help. Neither does being a professional actor or living in one of the most expensive cities in the world, New York.

The truth is, we're all working to find our way through this strange period of establishing our independence and identity in an economic environment where the odds feel stacked against us. And to make matters worse, we're making easily avoidable financial blunders that make it even harder—continually sacrificing the fruits of tomorrow for the indulgences of today.

So I'm searching for the balance. I want to retire someday, but not at the cost of giving up every pleasure and whim of the present. And I want to enjoy the here and now, but not for the price of my future. Regardless of my current circumstances, I'm determined to achieve financial freedom and live a glorious and beautiful life on my way to getting there.

So that's what this book is about—the journey. Navigating the chasm between everything that I want and need, and the funds to support it.

I hope my personal journey will serve as either guidance, brilliance, stupidity, entertainment, or just assurance that you're not alone in your "brokeness." I'm off to live the broke and beautiful life, with the hope that someday soon, the broke will become the abundant for you and me both.

CHAPTER 1

Pursue Your Passion

You've probably heard it a million times—"do what you love," "love what you do," or some incarnation thereof. I don't know how you can commit to working forty-plus years doing a job that doesn't spark *some* kind of excitement or passion in you. Reconciling what you love to do with how you're going to pay your bills, that's the tricky part.

So what should we do? Give up on our dreams and settle for a decent paycheck? Or blindly do what we love, even if it doesn't pay our bills?

Either option is a recipe for some form of misery—professional, personal, or financial—so let me offer some suggestions for fulfilling your professional goals with consideration for your bank account.

How to Pursue Your Passion *and* Pay Your Bills

Whatever your passion is, throw yourself into it 100 percent. Improve your skill set, knowledge, and marketability—do what you need to do to become the best that you can be at what it is you want to do.

You can't resign to failing at something if you never committed to mastering it.

Now, I'm not under the delusion that classes, networking opportunities, events, etc., come free. They take time and money, both of which are scarce and valuable. But the sacrifice is only temporary. Remember, you're committing to your dream, and a career fueled by passion is the ultimate reward.

Don't be afraid to look for unconventional ways to seize growth opportunities. Could you barter a class in return for assisting the teacher? Could you get free entry into a conference by helping with the setup or breakdown?

Don't let your wildest dreams be deterred by something as small as an entry fee. Channel your passion into finding ways to overcome the obstacles of your limited resources. Make *your* dreams happen in a way that works with *your* financial reality.

Commit to Financial Literacy

Learning how to make your money work for you in the most efficient and effective way possible will afford you the freedom to pursue your greatest goals.

By practicing financial literacy, you will free up many of the resources—time and money being chief among them—that you would otherwise have to use just to "get by."

For those of you wondering what I mean by *financial literacy,* I'm talking common sense money management— knowing how to handle your dollars and cents in the day to day, and how to prepare for a long and healthy financial future.

Reduce Expenses to Live within Your Means

The less money that you have to spend to meet your basic costs of living, the less time you have to spend on work that doesn't serve you, your dreams, or your passion. There will be more on the *how* of reducing your cost of living later, but for now, understanding the *why*—when you have to turn down an invite to happy hour or resist the temptation to drop in on your favorite store—will be instrumental in getting you to your end goal.

Develop Your Skill Set

If you have an in-demand, specialized skill like web coding, tailoring, or carpentry, you will find that you have much more flexibility in finding work to supplement your income during the pursuit of your dream job or passion project.

Practical skills are always in demand. As a supplier of such skills, you can charge a premium for your work and set a schedule that serves your priorities best. Those of us without such skills, myself included, are limited to the more conventional "survival" jobs, the ones that almost anyone can do. As such, it's harder to negotiate for better pay or more flexible hours. Without a specialized skill, you're much more likely to be replaced than accommodated.

A freelance web designer, for instance, is able to command a significantly higher hourly rate and much more flexible schedule, than say, a waiter. If you don't have some kind of skill that can help you better leverage your time for money, consider cultivating one, so that you can devote more energy to your top priorities rather than working all hours of the day just to scrape by.

Allow Your Priorities to Change with Your Passion

When you find your calling, it's hard to imagine doing anything else or having another aspect of your life become more important, but be open to that possibility. Don't fall into perpetual unhappiness by allowing what was once your dream or passion to blind you to who you are now and what you want in the present. Dreams and passions change, and priorities should change with them. Allow your plans to evolve as you do.

If the pursuit of your dream job, or even your dream job itself, is not reflecting your joy, take the time to rediscover what you want and prioritize with those new goals in mind.

What If You Don't Have a Passion?

Of course, not everyone has an intense passion or a crystal clear dream. Some of us are merely floating in space, not knowing which direction to go, and waiting for some kind of gravitational pull to guide us. Unfortunately, existing anywhere, be it laser focused on an end goal or floating through space trying to "find yourself," costs money, so many of the steps are going to remain the same—commit to financial literacy, keep your cost of living down, and develop skills that allow you to bring in survival income on your own terms.

When trying to identify your passion, look for work that aligns with who you are. This may sound like a heady concept, but it's quite simple. What are your strengths as a person? Communication? Creativity? Organization? If your friends or colleagues were asked, what would *they* say are your greatest skills? Then look for ways to harness those skills into a career that serves you and the things most important to you—a certain work environment, a particular lifestyle, potential for growth, etc.

Don't Settle for Misery

Regardless of whether you've identified your passion or not, don't get stuck in "comfortable misery." Committing to a career that doesn't interest you today is to set yourself up for unhappiness in the future. The longer you wait to make a change, the more likely you are to resign yourself to a lifetime of unhappiness with your chosen career.

Major financial commitments may seem far away now, but they will come sooner than you imagine. With a mortgage or family to support, taking the risk of unemployment or a pay cut in order to pursue your dream will be daunting enough to deter you from even trying. Take the big risks *now*!

The Danger of Doing What You Love

As bleak as a passionless life may sound, know that there are dangers to doing what you love for a living, as well. I should know, I'm a professional actress... *I've lived it.*

At age twenty-one, I had just graduated from New York University with degrees in psychology and theatre when I secured a job on a yearlong Asian tour for the musical *Cinderella*. I was understudying one of my professional idols. I still remember my first few days of work; I sat in rehearsals, pinching myself, not believing that my dreams were coming true.

A few months later, the Great Recession of 2008 hit, and a few months after that, my dream job was cut short. I went back to New York to "pound the pavement" and find my next gig. I was optimistic. Between my fresh-out-of-college naiveté and the major acting credit on my resume, I figured I'd be back to working my dream job in no time.

About a month later I got my first bitter taste of the acting profession that I had come to love. I was offered a contract to play three principal roles in three musicals for $225 per week. In addition to rehearsals and performances, I would be expected to contribute to other technical elements of the show—sets, costumes, etc. Mind you, this was not a summer job between semesters in college. Yes, I was young, but this was my *living*.

I decided to turn down the offer. Instead, I took a lucrative job as a singer on a cruise ship, which I absolutely hated. Although the job paid well, it made me miserable, and I quit after two months.

I spent the following year working quite a bit; first at a regional theatre, then on the road with a touring show. I was happy performing, but every contract I negotiated felt like I was giving up more and more just to continue living my dream. Less pay, no benefits, and horrible working conditions became the norm.

I was on a tour where we would get on a bus at 5 a.m., drive until 4 p.m., check into a hotel, and then drive to the theatre for a 5 p.m. sound check. That was followed by an evening performance, ending sometime around midnight. This continued day after day. It got to the point where every other aspect of my life was secondary. I felt like I was giving up everything to continue working my "dream" that continued to take from me.

But then it happened, my big break...or so I thought. I was called in as a last minute replacement for a major show. I didn't know much about the contract other than the fact that I was going to be performing in a multi-million dollar musical at Madison Square Garden! It was thrilling. I jumped in and learned the show in two days. I was so enthralled with the production that I didn't think twice about contract details or pay. I was in love.

And then it came, $542 per week (before taxes, union dues, and agent fees). This couldn't be right. I had *made it.* But as I calculated my financial reality, I realized that in four weeks I'd only take home $1,600. If you know anything about New York City living, then you know that $1,600 per month doesn't quite cut it. What had I allowed myself to do financially simply because I was so in love with my work?

I loved that job. And I would do it again. And therein lies the danger for people who love what they do. They are willing to compromise everything, even their ability to afford basic living expenses, to continue doing what they love. The irony is, if we negotiate the things that we need as human beings—proper and fair payment being chief among them—then we often lose our freedom to pursue the life and career that we love.

Finding a Balance

While I believe strongly in finding engaging and stimulating work, I have also learned that there is more to consider beyond a job itself: sustainable income, work-life balance, time commitment, and potential for growth need to be considered, too. Fulfillment comes in many ways, and it's not always in turning your passion into income.

But if you have a dream, give it a shot. Give it 100 percent. Live it and love it until what you want the most changes. When you love stability more, when you love money more, when you love anything else *more*, you should reprioritize and pursue those ends.

Stephen Colbert said it best in his commencement address to the Northwestern University graduates of 2011.

"Thankfully, dreams can change. If we'd all stuck with our first dream, the world would be overrun with cowboys and princesses. So whatever your dream is right now, if you don't achieve it, you haven't failed and you're not some loser..."

Follow your dreams, but don't be limited by them.

Empowerment

Regardless of what dream you're pursuing, there will be many factors, obstacles, and influences beyond your control. It's the most frustrating reality I've come to learn about the "real world."

Throughout your many years of education, you learned to follow a "recipe" of sorts—if you do A, B, and C, then you'll get result D. If you do your homework, turn in assignments on time, and study hard, you'll be rewarded with success.

But when you get into the practical, real life application of that recipe—implementing A, B, and C, only to find out that you're getting nowhere—it's frustrating. You build your professional network, apply for jobs, and take classes to improve your skills, and yet, you remain unemployed. Why?

Things aren't always cause and effect, and equal efforts don't necessarily produce equal results. Career trajectories often feel more like a roller coaster than a linear progression. Trying to understand all of the factors outside your control will make your head spin.

But what you *can* do is empower yourself by mastering the things that you *can* control. And what better tool is there to seize control and empower yourself than money? What affords you more opportunities than the mastery and growth of your personal finances? What opens the door to the pursuit of dreams more than financial freedom?

CHAPTER 2

Money Mentality

Ever have one of those moments when it comes to managing your finances when you want to let out an angry scream or a defeated cry? We've all been there. When problems arise, there's a tendency to react in one of two ways. The first is to wallow, stewing in self-pity and crippling inaction. The second is to have a strong, emotional response, which rarely leads to good decision making. To effectively deal with these moments, action needs to be taken as a result of calculated, rational thinking, rather than a knee-jerk emotional response. These ineffective responses are generally a result of our upbringing, experiences, and formative money moments.

Formative Money Moments

We all have a tendency to get locked into a certain way of approaching our finances—sometimes positive, sometimes negative, and often in patterns that are not conducive to smart money management. In working to develop your new, positive money mentality, it's helpful to identify what created your initial thought patterns about money in the first place. When you hold on tightly to your early experiences, rather than adapting to the reality of the present, you'll find that your strategies—financial or otherwise—don't serve you as effectively as they could.

Expectations of our respective financial futures are often learned from the examples around us, namely friends and family. Our parents' attitudes and beliefs about money become ingrained in our own money mentality and manifest themselves in our own actions—the way we shop, the way we save money, how we measure success, and so on. Now, if your parents were money rock stars, then you're in luck. But if money was ever a struggle in your household, then adopting a positive money mentality will likely be a struggle for you.

If you find yourself constantly broke and struggling to manage your money, perhaps it's time to take a second look at your habits and see if the mindset behind them is still serving you—or if, perhaps, you could benefit from some newer and more functional monetary understandings.

The Power of Example

I spent my childhood surrounded by people who fully realized the American Dream. My grandparents fled to the United States after World War II with nothing but my ten-year-old aunt in tow. A year later my mother was born, and six years after that, her father died unexpectedly. Despite the challenges of being raised in a single parent home, facing a language barrier and poverty, my aunt and mother worked hard and secured scholarships to Ivy League universities—paving the way for their unprecedented success in their respective fields. Their friends and neighbors, also immigrants and children of immigrant families, followed the same trajectory. So when it came time for me to plan my future, I never questioned that I was capable of success.

I've always felt that my possibilities were limitless, not only because I've been given the resources and opportunities to pursue my dreams, but because I have such remarkable examples of success in my day-to-day life. It never occurred to me that the expectations I had become accustomed to were lower, or even non-existent, elsewhere in the United States—"the land of opportunity." But in my years of touring the country as a performer, I've come across many people, even entire communities, constricted by their own ideas of what's possible.

We've come to define the "glass ceiling" largely as a limitation for women and minorities in the white, male-dominated, Corporate America. But I've found that glass ceilings can also be self-imposed, based largely on our own expectations, personal experiences, culture, and family.

For instance, if you come from a small town or a culture where women are still thought of as homemakers and caretakers, and you don't have exposure to different kinds of people with different career paths, then how do you know that alternatives exist? Similarly, if you're surrounded by constant monetary struggle, how will you know the actions required to break that financial mindset? How will you know that money can be *freeing* rather than a constant burden and source of frustration?

The Power of Experience

Formative money moments not only come in the form of observations and examples set by friends and family, but they also come from our own experiences, too.

After graduating from college, I was lucky to have my full-time dream job waiting for me. I spent seven of the best months of my life performing throughout Asia, banking my entire salary and living off a generous per diem. But this made the reality of coming back to the states, facing unemployment, and getting my first real taste of adulthood in the middle of a severe recession all the more jarring. For the first time, I wasn't protected by my parents' roof or my college "plan." There was no more per diem, just unemployment and, thankfully, my previous salary that I had managed to save. It was during this first year of "real life" that I had two major money revelations.

Revelation #1: Life Is Expensive.

Have you ever been uninsured? Do you remember the first time you saw how much health insurance costs? I think I had cartoon eyes bulging out of my head when I first saw the numbers! Needless to say, I was without health insurance for five years—thank goodness for Planned Parenthood, which provided me with a free full examination every year (I know who's getting my money when I'm rich and famous).

But it wasn't just the cost of health insurance that struck me when I started paying my own bills, it was *everything*. All of the things that I had taken for granted as a child—the endless types of insurance (who knew there were so many disasters to prepare for?), transportation, home furnishings, and the cumulative cost of basic necessities like cleaning supplies and toilet paper.

If it weren't for the fact that I was unemployed, I may not have been fazed by all of these expenses, but I hated seeing all of my hard earned money slowly dissipate in order to fund the mundane expenses of life.

Revelation #2: Pursuing Your Passion Is Tough Stuff.

My second major money moment came when I was offered my second professional acting job. I had recently returned from touring and had been unemployed and auditioning for about two months. In terms of being an actor, the turnover wasn't too bad, but the offer was—$225 per week.

Guess what happened when I heard the offer? Cartoon eyes again! This was a professional theatre, not a stage to perform as a hobby. How could the company expect me to accept so little money? My unemployment check was for more!

While both of these revelations left me upset and defeated at the time, the power of these formative financial experiences was instrumental in shaping my perception of money—thankfully, in a way that inspired me to make smart financial decisions and change my money mentality.

But the same experiences of unemployment and underpayment through a negative lens could have led to an entirely different mindset. I could have used my limited income as an excuse to stay trapped in a cycle of never having enough. Rather than seeking out additional employment opportunities, high powered savings vehicles, and frugal alternatives on everything from groceries to getaways, I could have resigned myself to the thought that the world isn't fair, doesn't value me or what I do, and therefore I'll have to scrape by forever. Instead, I chose to screw on a positive lens, give thanks for everything that I *did* have, and let those things empower me.

What's Your Money Mindset?

Between the monetary examples you witnessed in your youth and your formative financial experiences, what has *your* monetary mindset evolved to be? Is it positive or negative? Is it serving you?

What actions can you take to start implementing a positive money mentality and constructive patterns of money management?

Continuing a cycle of negative thoughts will do nothing to improve your finances. In fact, it will only reinforce your negative experiences, creating more panic and less ability to solve your problems. You can continue to become frustrated and make excuses for not changing or taking action, or you can start implementing positivity and make the transition from whining to winning.

Practice every day to root out your old negative patterns of thinking and behavior. What we tell ourselves about our world and our money is the foundation of our happiness and prosperity, so let's make it something rich!

CHAPTER 3

——— ·•· ———

Financial Building Blocks

I remember one afternoon in my early twenties, feeling responsible and adult-like, I picked up a copy of *The Wall Street Journal.* I had just graduated from college with a hundred thousand dollar education, and I was reduced to feeling like a first grader in a matter of seconds. A few sentences into an article on recent stock market performance and I felt as though I was reading another language.

Thirteen years in the public school system and an additional four years at a top university did little, or rather, nothing to prepare me for basic financial realities. Forget *Wall Street Journal* fanciness, I'm talking A, B, Cs...

- How do I budget?
- How do taxes work?
- What is a credit score? Do I have one? Does it matter?
- Do I need a credit card?
- How should I pay down my debt?
- How much money should I be saving?
- What is a stock? What is a bond? What's a good investment?

- Retirement? Do I need to start doing something about that?

There were many more questions that I didn't even know to ask. I had no financial foundation, no financial vocabulary, and no financial literacy.

You can't do algebra if you don't know basic arithmetic. Similarly, your money won't work for you if you don't understand financial fundamentals.

No wonder so many otherwise intellectual adults toss their paychecks into low-yielding checking accounts, buy houses with mortgages they can't afford, and throw money away leasing depreciating cars—they don't know any better!

Money management is possibly the most practical and necessary skill to be learned and yet it's completely passed over in the educational system. If we take the responsibility to educate *ourselves,* however, we can not only avoid financial pitfalls, but *prosper,* both intellectually and fiscally.

The Building Blocks of Financial Literacy

1. How to Spend
2. How to Save
3. How to Pay Down Debt
4. How to Build Credit
5. How to Grow Your Money and Plan for Retirement
6. Get Started!

Building Block #1: How to Spend

You're probably thinking, "Spending isn't my problem, I *know* how to spend." But there's a big difference between *spending* and *conscious, thoughtful* spending. It's the difference between buying things that you want versus things that you need, and recognizing when you can afford to do one, both, or neither.

Conscious Spending: Where Does It All Go?

Money seems to dissipate at an unprecedented pace—at least in my life. By the time I've paid my rent, bought groceries, and accounted for transportation for the month, it feels like I'm back at zero.

A few years ago I decided to take charge of my finances by writing down every dollar and cent that I spent. When you see your spending laid out in front of you like that, you gain perspective and learn something about yourself—*you learn what you value most.*

How to Align Your Spending with Your Values

We'd all like to believe that we're spending money in a way that reflects our priorities and values, but so many of us continue to rack up unnecessary charges in the form of clothing, booze, and vacations while we put off paying down our mortgage, student loans, and credit cards. Do we really value these trivial fleeting indulgences more than the roof over our head? If you're reviewing your finances and finding that your spending doesn't reflect your priorities, it's time to reassess by following four simple steps.

Step 1: List your priorities in descending order.

Consider the following categories:
- Bare-bones necessities: food and shelter
- Day-to-day tools: phone, Internet

- Support categories: heat, hot water, electricity, transportation, insurance
- Life expenses: doctor visits, basic personal care products
- Business support expenses: resume printing, classes, web hosting
- Social expenses: gifts, dinner with friends, correspondence
- Luxuries: new clothes, massages, vacations

Step 2: Compare your list with your actual spending.

Review your pattern of spending over the last few months. Have you included everything? Look through credit card statements and receipts to be sure. Has your spending reflected the order of priorities outlined in Step 1? This exercise can illuminate important areas of your life that you may be neglecting in favor of other, more trivial, expenses.

Step 3: Find your balance.

It's important to find the balance between what you value and what you allocate money towards. If a high percentage of your spending is going towards luxuries at the expense of other categories (like life expenses or day-to-day tools), perhaps it's time to strike a better balance.

Step 4: Remember, we all have different priorities.

Did you purchase a new pair of cute shoes before paying off the dental cleaning you charged to your credit card last month? That's fine if you value style more than health. No one can tell you what you should or shouldn't value above anything else. Just be true to yourself by keeping your spending in line with the priorities you've laid out in Step 1.

Tracking your spending not only helps bring value to your priorities, but it also brings value to your money in general. Every penny earned should be valued as much as the time spent to earn it, and every penny spent should be valued as much as the item, service, or purpose for which it is used. With that kind of respect for your time and money, you're more likely to value each and every purchase. As a result, you'll make smarter financial decisions. That's what I call *conscious spending.*

Building Block #2: How to Save

Saving money is something that neither you nor I can afford to continually compromise. In addition to funding future purchases, savings serve as the buffer between you and debt. If you spend all that you earn each month without setting anything aside for emergencies, you leave yourself vulnerable to credit card reliance and high interest debt. Even if you're young and seemingly invincible, the fact is, you're at risk.

A few years back, I went to get a loose crown checked at the dentist. It quickly turned into a $250 tooth extraction, and sheer panic set in as I thought about the $1,800 dental implant that would follow. Examples like this are why having an *emergency fund* is essential.

An emergency fund is not for taking a vacation or buying another new phone. Instead, it's the money you'll use when you lose your job, need to fix your leaky roof, or need to pay medical bills when your teeth, bones, or any other body part gives out on you.

The sad reality is that something unexpected and expensive is *going* to happen. You are not immune. So if you're thinking, "I can't afford to have an emergency fund," start thinking, "I can't afford *not* to." Those who don't have emergency funds are more likely to amass debt. No savings equals no buffer. Start saving now before you find yourself in a hole you can never get out of.

How Much Do I Need?

Experts recommend setting aside anywhere from $1,000 to nine months of living expenses for your emergency fund. The thought that I would have an extra nine months of living expenses just lying around is as laughable to me as it probably is to all the broke and beautiful—so let me offer my suggestion.

Open a high-yield savings account with an initial deposit of $1,000 to start. If you don't have $1,000, find a way to get it—take a second job, babysit, sell items on eBay, etc. While $1,000 is a good start, it isn't going to get you very far in case of an emergency—so once you've made your initial deposit, contribute weekly, bi-weekly, or monthly to your emergency fund until you've built a nice cushion—preferably enough to cover three to six months of living expenses.

How Do I Start Saving?

If you're having trouble saving, consider setting up direct deposit into your emergency account. If you tend to spend impulsively, forgo the debit card attached to the account. While your emergency money needs to be accessible (not tied up in a retirement account or risked in the stock market), you don't want it to be so readily available that you blow it all on the new iPhone with one swipe of plastic.

To ensure that your emergency account is being continually funded, consider automating a small deposit from each paycheck into the account until you've reached your savings goal. Start with an amount that seems negligible—for instance, 2 percent of each paycheck—and try to slowly increase the percentage over time. Even small, seemingly negligible contributions can make a meaningful difference in building your savings buffer, and with an automatic deposit in place, you probably won't even miss the money from your paycheck.

Building Block #3: How to Pay Down Debt

Whether it's "good" debt like a student loan or mortgage, or "bad" debt like a high interest consumer loan, debt has the potential to bury you financially and emotionally under its crushing weight. If you've already amassed a considerable amount of debt, follow these five steps to begin your journey toward debt repayment.

Step 1: Take responsibility for your debt.

The more blame you place on circumstances and factors outside your control, the more time you waste pointing fingers rather than taking action, and the more power you give up to make a change.

Taking full responsibility for your debt is not only difficult, but it can make you feel depressed, angry, and a whole host of other negative emotions that won't serve you. Recognize that your debt is merely a reflection of bad thinking and bad habits *in your past.* Empower yourself and your finances by committing to a brighter and better financial future.

Step 2: Identify how you got here.

Think back on the choices you made that led you to your debt debacle. Did you live beyond your means? Did you have an expensive medical emergency? Did you pursue higher education without a plan to pay for it?

Once you identify and accept the choices that led to your debt, you can identify the thought processes and habits that led to those actions, and you can begin finding ways to break them.

Step 3: Replace old habits with new ones.

For every bad, debt producing habit in your past, map out a new, constructive alternative. For example, if you had a tendency to live beyond your means and buy more than you could afford, develop a new approach for shopping and paying regular expenses. Consider switching to a "cash-only" system, with specific amounts of money set aside for each expense category.

Step 4: Set goals.

Make a list of positive goals to motivate you on your debt repayment journey. Don't forget to celebrate every little step in the right direction. You had to take responsibility for your poor choices, so don't forget to celebrate your good ones!

Step 5: Develop a debt repayment strategy.

When trying to pay off a huge sum of debt, the sheer magnitude of the total balance can make you feel hopeless and afraid to begin. Rather than avoiding and ignoring your debt, be proactive by creating a debt repayment plan.

I prefer the popular approach known as the *"Debt Snowball."* Here's how it works:

1. Begin by listing all of your debts and the total amounts owed.
2. Put them in ascending order from the smallest debt to the largest.
3. Commit to making the minimum monthly payment on all debts.
4. Calculate how much additional money you can contribute toward paying off your debt, after satisfying all minimum payments, and apply that amount to the smallest debt until it is paid off.
5. Take the full amount that was being contributed to the smallest debt and start chipping away at the next smallest debt, all the while making minimum payments on all of your debts.
6. Continue this "snowball," never reducing the total amount paid, until all debt has been paid off.

Debt Snowball Example...

- Credit card bill: $400 ($50 minimum monthly payment)
- Medical bill: $1,000 ($30 minimum monthly payment)
- Car loan: $6,000 ($100 minimum monthly payment)
- Student loan: $10,000 ($120 minimum monthly payment)

To implement the debt snowball on this hypothetical debt load, you would commit to making the minimum monthly payment on all four debts, which totals $300 per month.

Let's assume that after making the $300 per month minimum payments, you have an additional $100 available to pay down your debt. The entire $100 would go towards paying off the smallest debt first, which in this case is the credit card bill. Therefore, a total of $150 is going towards paying off the credit card bill.

Once the credit card bill is paid off, the $150 per month that was being applied to that payment now gets applied to the medical bill, *on top of* the minimum payment you're already making. This means that you're paying a total of $180 per month towards the medical bill while continuing to pay the minimums on the car and student loans.

Once the medical bill is paid off, that $180 per month is applied to the car loan, raising that monthly payment to $280—again, maintaining the minimum payment on the student loan. Once the car loan is paid off, all $400 per month gets applied to the student loan.

The psychology behind the debt snowball is simple. *The momentum of paying off the smaller debts first will carry over into making progress on the larger payments.* By starting with your small bills, you will see progress sooner, motivating you to continue.

Of course, mathematically speaking, the debt snowball isn't the most logical option. Some experts would argue that you should start paying off the debt with the highest interest rate first. It will take longer for you to see tangible progress using this strategy, but it's the most cost effective in the long run.

Ultimately, if you have an action plan for your debt and you're paying more than the minimum each month, you're taking the right steps toward eliminating your debt. Sticking to a strategy that works for *you* is what's most important.

Building Block #4: How to Build Credit

You've probably seen the barrage of "free credit report" commercials on television, but do you actually know what a credit score is? Your credit score, often referred to as your FICO score (the Fair Isaac Corporation, the most popular credit score calculation), is a measure of how well you borrow money. In other words, it's a number that tells lenders how likely you are to pay back a loan.

Your credit score isn't only a deciding factor in being approved for (or denied) financing, but it's also used as a measure of trustworthiness in seemingly unrelated aspects of your life. Everyone from potential employers to landlords to insurance companies may be using your credit score to assess your responsibility and reliability.

How Is It Calculated?

Your credit score is calculated based on the information found in your credit reports, as provided by the three major credit bureaus—Experian, Equifax, and TransUnion. The weighted average of the following five categories is used to determine your credit score.

- **Payment History (35%)**
  Have you paid your past credit accounts on time? This is the most heavily weighted part of your credit score and is determined by repayment of past debt. If you have multiple late or missed payments, your score will suffer.

- **Amounts Owed (30%)**
  What percentage of available credit are you currently using? Your utilization ratio is your total amount of debt compared to your amount of available credit. While experts recommend keeping your utilization ratio under 30 percent, the less you owe, the better.

- **Length of Credit History (15%)**
  How long have your credit accounts been established? The longer your credit history, the better. Avoid canceling your oldest credit cards (unless they carry annual fees), as they help this portion of your credit score.

- **New Credit (10%)**
  Have you opened several new credit accounts in a short period of time? Opening multiple new accounts in a short period of time can damage your credit score because it suggests that you are desperate to borrow and have trouble managing debt.

- **Types of Credit Used (10%)**
  Do you have a mix of credit cards, retail accounts, and loans? Having a variety of credit—revolving, installment, and open—can boost your score. Revolving credit (credit cards) refers to accounts that require a different payment each month depending on the current balance.

Installment credit (mortgage and student loans) refers to loans that have a fixed payment for a fixed period of time. Open credit (utilities and cell phone) refers to accounts that have no credit limit and a variable balance, but require you to pay the full balance each month.

What Does Your Number Mean?

Your credit score can range from 350 to 850. The generally used score brackets and their respective designations are as follows:

- 750-850: Excellent
- 660-749: Good
- 620-659: Fair
- 350-619: Poor

If you have no credit history, you may be a "zero," which means you'll probably have trouble being approved for any kind of financing, even a basic credit card.

Fun (or not so fun) fact: Even if you earn a six figure salary and have significant savings in your bank account, no credit history still makes you a risk to lenders by traditional credit reporting standards. Credit is determined by how well you *borrow,* not by how much you *earn.*

How to Improve Your Credit Score

To increase your credit score, you need to create a history of financial stability and responsible borrowing. To achieve this, consider the following strategies.

Build Your Credit. If you have no credit history then you have no score, therefore you'll have trouble being approved for a loan—yes, it's a catch-22. To begin building credit, consider opening a secured credit card through your bank or credit union. Banks offer secured credit cards more easily than unsecured cards because an up-front deposit serves as collateral. Your credit limit will be equal to the initial deposit you make with the bank. If you don't pay off your balance, then the bank keeps your deposit. Once you establish a consistent record of paying off your secured credit card balance each month, you should be able to transition to an unsecured credit card.

Pay Your Bills on Time. It's as basic as it gets. Pay your bills on time and in full to improve your credit score.

Don't Use All of Your Available Credit. Keep your credit utilization below the 30 percent mark. This means that you should carry no more than $300 worth of charges at any given time if your credit card limit is $1,000.

Check Your Credit Reports for Accuracy. Unfortunately, mistakes on credit reports are common and their effects can be quite costly when it comes to determining your score and subsequent interest rates for loans. Federal law mandates your right to receive a free credit report annually, however, this *does not* mean that you are entitled to a free credit score. Luckily, there are credit monitoring services that offer free trial memberships and allow you to check your score. Just be sure to cancel your trial before you get hit with a hefty subscription fee.

Building Block #5: How to Grow Your Money and Plan for Retirement

Hiding cash under your mattress or keeping your entire net worth in a checking account earning little interest isn't going to help you or your nest egg. Determine how much cash you need on hand to cover your basic living expenses and split the rest between a high-yield savings account and your retirement portfolio.

Know the Demands of Your Money

Before you can plan for any kind of financial future, or financial present for that matter, you need to know exactly what you have to work with. What is your income and where is it going? Start tracking everything that you earn and everything that you spend to get an exact picture of your current financial demands and what assets will be available for your future financial planning.

Based on those figures, you can determine an amount or percentage that you can comfortably set aside for retirement contributions each month. Saving 10 percent of your income is a standard recommendation, but with an entry-level salary and major monetary demands like student loan payments, it's okay to start smaller and increase your contributions when you're able.

Even if you can only contribute a small percentage of each paycheck to your retirement accounts, it's important to develop the habit of setting aside money for your future. When it comes to saving for retirement, time can be far more valuable than money, thanks to the wonderful effects of compound interest.

Let's use an example to see how powerful the union of compound interest and time can be. If you begin saving for retirement at age twenty-five, setting aside just $38 of your weekly paycheck, or about $2,000 per year, you'll have over $500,000 in forty years, assuming an 8 percent annual rate of return. But if you wait just ten years, until you're thirty-five years old, to implement the *same* savings strategy of contributing $2,000 per year to your retirement accounts with the same rate of return, you'll have less than $250,000 when you reach age sixty-five—that's less than half! Time is money—literally!

Know the Basics

The general rule is that you can't withdraw money from your retirement accounts before age 59½ without incurring a penalty. While you want to contribute as much as possible towards retirement, be sure to save money for short-term savings goals elsewhere. As for which types of retirement accounts you should fund with your contributions, I recommend a 401(k) and Roth IRA.

Many employers offer 401(k) retirement account matches as part of their benefits package. This means that however much you contribute to your 401(k), your employer will match a certain percentage of those contributions, up to a given threshold. Both the percentage and the threshold vary depending on the employer, but any kind of match is essentially free money, so make the most of it!

Once you've maximized your 401(k) employer match (or if your employer doesn't offer a 401(k) plan), start contributing to a Roth IRA (Individual Retirement Account). All contributions to a Roth IRA are made with after-tax dollars, but you can withdraw the principal and investment earnings tax-free when you reach age 59½.

Choose Your Investments Wisely

An important element to understand about Roth IRA and 401(k) accounts is that they are simply holding accounts. Once you open the account and make a contribution, you'll have to choose investments to own *within* the account.

Mention the word "investment" and most young adults tune out, thinking they're in over their heads. But the truth is, investing can be kept simple and still provide a favorable return. How so? Index funds. I won't get into the monotonous, boring details, but selecting a few high-quality index funds is a simple and cost effective solution for many investors.

The hardest part of implementing any new habit is getting started. When it comes to retirement planning, where time *really is money*, procrastination can mean missing out on thousands, if not hundreds of thousands of dollars. My mission isn't to teach you to invest, I'll leave that to the pros. My mission is to get you to increase your financial literacy so you can feel confident managing your money. Take free online classes at Morningstar.com's *Investing Classroom*, visit Khan Academy online and watch the introductory personal finance videos—do everything you can to build your confidence, and then harness that confidence to start making your cash work smarter for *you*.

Building Block #6: Get Started!

You've been provided with the outline, and now it's up to you to fill it in. Create a plan that works for your goals, priorities, and circumstances. Establish an understanding and a vocabulary for handling the language of finance and investing that works for *you*. By constantly learning—expanding your vocabulary and mastering the concepts—you're setting yourself up for success.

CHAPTER 4

———•———

Conscious Spending

I have a confession to make…I want it all! I want to travel the world and I want to afford a down payment on a home. I want to retire comfortably someday and I want to enjoy the occasional Starbucks today. I want to keep my spending in line with my priorities and I want to enjoy trivial indulgences. I want to fulfill my long-term needs and I want to entertain my fleeting wants. Enter, *budgets.*

If you want to have it all, you need to create a budget. You may think that a budget is restrictive, but by helping you prioritize your resources, a budget serves as the ultimate tool for giving you everything that you want and need now and in the future.

Without a specific plan for your finances, your dreams of owning a home, living in the big (or small) city, traveling the world, dining in fine restaurants, and pursuing your passions, will remain just that, dreams. A budget is the road map for getting you from where you are now to where you need to be financially in order to fulfill your goals. Rather than turning a blind eye to your finances and remaining in a world full of wishes, take action by employing one of these budget strategies.

The Zero-Sum Budget

The zero-sum budget designates a place and purpose for every dollar you earn. As opposed to funding necessities and spending what's left over whimsically, the zero-sum budget dictates the ultimate destination for all of your earnings. Follow these five steps to create a zero-sum budget.

Step 1: Calculate how much you earn in a given month.

How many paychecks will you receive and how much will each check amount to? If you're not receiving a consistent salary, get in the habit of using last month's income to pay for this month's expenses. This will ensure that you're working with accurate numbers rather than estimates.

Step 2: Pay yourself first.

Make all contributions to debt repayment, savings, and investments at the *beginning* of the month rather than at the end. This prevents you from spending that money elsewhere before the month's end.

Step 3: Calculate mandatory expenses for the month.

This should include everything from monthly bills like your mortgage, utilities, and groceries, to quarterly and other intermittent payments like insurance premiums and property taxes.

Step 4: Designate a purpose for all leftover money.

After accounting for all of your necessary expenses, you'll know exactly how much you have left over to spend at your discretion. You can use this money to finance your "wants" like entertainment and vacations, or set aside additional funds for debt repayment, savings, and investment goals. I recommend a combination of both.

Step 5: Track your spending.

Carefully track your spending throughout the month to see how reality compares to your goals. By listing everything that you've spent money on, you'll be able to make adjustments as necessary.

The Cash Envelope Budget

The envelope budgeting system uses cash limits to control spending. Paying with cash has proven to result in less spending than mindless credit card swiping. The physical nature of cash also creates a tangible limit as to how much you have available to spend and prevents you from exceeding that limit. A cash envelope budget can be created in four steps.

Step 1: Create your categories.

The cash envelope budget requires you to divide your expenses into categories. Create a category for everything from groceries to savings to trips to your favorite restaurant.

Step 2: Create an envelope for each category.

Purchase envelopes large enough to hold cash but small enough to fit into your purse or wallet. Write the name of each category on a separate envelope—food, entertainment, transportation, etc.

Step 3: Fill the envelopes.

Each monthly spending category should have a respective envelope filled with the designated cash limit. For example, $300 budgeted for groceries means that you should put $300 cash into the grocery envelope. Recurring monthly payments, like your mortgage or emergency fund contributions, can be represented by empty reminder envelopes.

Step 4: Withdraw cash from each envelope as needed.

After withdrawing cash from an envelope in order to make a payment, write down how much is left on the back of the envelope so that you have a running tab of how much cash remains for the month. When you run out of cash in an envelope, you can choose to either not spend any more on that category, or you can transfer cash from another envelope.

Percentage Budgeting

Rather than allocating strict dollar amounts to every line item in your budget, I recommend using a more flexible budgeting system called *percentage budgeting*. With this method, you will set a target percentage of your income to fund each expense category. For example, 55 percent of all income will go towards basic living expenses. You can include all of the regular line item budget categories—housing, transport, healthcare, etc.—or adopt a more general approach.

Percentage budgeting allows you the freedom to make simple trade-offs in your spending decisions. If you'd like to spend more in one category, you'll need to find another category where you're willing to cut back.

As someone with a highly variable income, percentage budgeting helps ensure that I'm continuing to fund *all* of my goals *all* of the time. For instance, when I receive a big paycheck, I don't think of it as one large sum. Rather, I divide it up by applying my percentages, and then decide how I'd like to spend it after seeing how much money has been allocated to each category.

For some unknown reason, additional or unexpected sources of income turn even fiscally responsible members of society into irrational spendthrifts. I'm not saying that you shouldn't spend *any* of your money on your desires, but try not to treat "extra" or "unexpected" cash any differently than you would treat any other paycheck or source of income. If you typically contribute a portion of each paycheck to your IRA, emergency fund, or student loan, do that with your "extra" money too. The new iPad or the cute boots that you've been itching to buy will still be there when you've saved enough money to buy them through proper budgeting.

Variations of the percentage budgeting system include the *Jars Money Management System*, the *60/20/20 Budget*, and the *Balanced Money Formula*.

The Jars Money Management System (by T. Harv Eker)
- 55% required expenses: housing, food, insurance payments, loan payments
- 10% savings: emergency fund contributions, contributions to short-term savings goals
- 10% financial freedom account: retirement contributions, stock purchases, money used to create passive income streams
- 10% education: taking classes, reading books, learning skills
- 10% play: vacations, nights out, entertainment
- 5% give: gifts and donations

60/20/20 Budget
- 60% required expenses
- 20% savings and future financial goals
- 20% splurge

Balanced Money Formula (by Elizabeth Warren)
- 50% required expenses
- 30% wants
- 20% savings and future financial goals

Percentage budgeting provides a guideline for living within your means. If you want to know how much you can afford to spend on basic necessities like housing, food, transportation, and insurance, assume 50 to 60 percent of your income. If you overload your required expenses beyond the 50 to 60 percent threshold, you won't have any money remaining for your wants and future goals. Percentage budgeting encourages you to keep your required expenses low so that you will have more flexibility to fund your wants and goals.

To keep your required expenses within 50 to 60 percent of your total income, you'll have to master the art of *conscious spending*. This is particularly true for low income earners. For example, if you only bring home $2,000 per month, you'll need to find a way to live on $1,000. If you're exceeding the 50 to 60 percent threshold, it's a sign that you need to reduce your cost of living or earn more.

The "Latte Factor"

If you've ever read about day-to-day money saving strategies, then you've probably heard of the "latte factor." In the most literal sense, the latte factor means ditching your daily coffee habit to save money. While it's true that $5 spent on Starbucks every day can add up to a considerable amount—$1,825 per year to be exact—it's important to recognize that the latte factor extends far beyond coffee.

The latte factor is a metaphor for the daily, weekly, monthly, and annual life luxuries we treat ourselves to without consideration for their cumulative cost. Here are a few versions of the "latte factor" you may be indulging in:

Movie Nights. These days, the cost of a movie ticket is outrageously expensive. Add in a 3D experience and a soft drink and you're looking at more than $20 per person. If you indulge in the full movie going experience twice a month, at $20 a pop, that's a "movie factor" of $480 per year.

Weekend Ragers. The weekend is a time to cut loose and relax, but not at the expense of your financial future. If you estimate five drinks per weekend at $7 each, plus tip, that's an annual "alcohol factor" of $1,820. That doesn't include additional expenses like bar covers, trans-portation, parking, and food.

Smoking. If the health risks weren't bad enough, consider that smoking one pack of cigarettes per week in New York City adds up to an annual "cigarette factor" of $624. If you smoke a pack of cigarettes per day, that number jumps to more than $4,380 per year!

Haircuts. A haircut every six weeks at $60 per cut plus tip will cost you around $650 per year. If you add in coloring, you'll more than double your "hair factor."

Events. According to American Express, the projected cost of attending one wedding in 2013 was $539. That includes travel, special attire, and accommodations. By the time you add up the cost of attending your high school reunion, two weddings, three birthday parties, and Thanksgiving at your parents' house, you could easily be looking at an annual "event factor" in the thousands of dollars.

These are just a few examples of the many versions of the latte factor that exist in our day-to-day lives. Once you identify what your "factors" are and how much they're costing you, you'll be able to decide if they're worth their cumulative price tag.

It's not just the *amount* of money spent on "latte factors" that can be problematic; it's *the habit* of spending consistently and unnecessarily. For example, there's an incredible little taqueria across the street from my apartment that makes me salivate in anticipation of eating one of their tacos. But at $3 a pop, they're not exactly budget friendly. Those delicious dishes are my personal latte factor. Sure, I *need* food, but I certainly don't *need* to get it in the form of gourmet tacos just because I'm feeling lazy or like I deserve a treat.

When purchases become automatic or emotional, and conscious spending is forgotten, your personal latte factor will quickly become a financial burden.

Conscious Spending Sabotage

I remember having a conversation with a colleague who had just moved to Central Park Towers, a luxury building right on Central Park West in Manhattan, i.e. my dream location if I had a million dollars. Considering that she, too, was an unemployed actress and we were having this conversation at an audition, I asked about the cost of her new home. At first I got a full lament about how expensive it was (not surprising, even if it was a studio apartment), and then I got a whole list of "yeah, buts..." The conversation went something like this...

Me: Could you get a roommate?
She: No, I have to live alone. My therapist says it's best for my mental health.
Me: Maybe a cheaper building?
She: I looked at all kinds of buildings with a realtor, there's nothing out there. I'm not going to live in a hell hole.
Me: Maybe a cheaper neighborhood?
She: I have to stay in Manhattan, all of my students and tutoring clients are on the Upper East/Upper West Side. It would be too far to commute.
Me: Could you make your commute time productive somehow, working on the train, reading, etc.?
She: No, I get motion sickness.

Me: How about staying in Manhattan, just in a more rea-
    sonably priced neighborhood like Inwood or Wash-
    ington Heights?
She: No, I hate it up there. It's too far.

The whole conversation could be summarized by this, "Yeah, I have a problem because I'm living in an apartment that I can't afford, but here's a list of reasons why I don't have any other choice."

I can give you a million ideas and ways to change your situation, but you have to be willing to do the work.

I found out that the rent on the Central Park Tower studio was $2,400 per month. I understand that finding an apartment in the big city with the perfect mix of location, cleanliness, safety, and price is difficult, but if you want to live in New York City for the long term, you have to be willing to make concessions and find a sustainable balance. The same is true of any challenge.

I used to live in Weehawken, New Jersey, a twenty-minute commute from Midtown Manhattan. The rent in my shared three-bedroom apartment was $500 per month. At the time I was commuting to Manhattan every day for auditions and for my work as a personal assistant and school administrator. Would it have been easier to live in Midtown Manhattan? Of course. Would it have been easier to come up with an extra $2,000 per month? Absolutely not.

What we perceive as being easier in the short term is often just avoidance of longer-term challenges. By not dealing with the long-term reality in the present, obstacles inevitably become more difficult. When you overspend for convenience, you sink into debt and risk damaging your credit when you fall behind on your bills. Excuses and avoidance are dangerous to your long-term financial health. You can continue to justify and "yeah, but" your way to zero, or you can take action and make a change.

The Urge to Splurge

Justifications and excuses are not the only spending pitfalls. Emotions also play a big part in conscious spending sabotage. Have you ever stopped to think about the way that you *feel* before making a purchase? Thinking about your state of being while spending may shed light on some of your less-than-ideal buying habits.

Here are a few examples of the emotional and situational triggers that can motivate a purchase. Perhaps if you recognize and raise your awareness of these triggers, you can combat those that are not serving you or your financial goals. When do you get the urge to splurge?

When Depressed. From being too lazy to cook and opting for takeout, to going on a shopping spree to create temporary satisfaction, depression can get expensive. Don't let your impulsive "depressed purchases" plunge you into debt and further despair. I'm not a licensed psychologist, but a walk outside or a phone date with a friend seems like a much better option than a credit card swipe.

To Motivate. How many people buy gym memberships and fancy new workout gear every January that have *yet* to set foot in a gym? When you get excited about something new, it can lead to a lot of preemptive spending. And while some of that may be necessary, if you don't follow through, it's just a waste of money. I can't tell you how many people I know that have spent a fortune on Rosetta Stone language learning software and have since abandoned the program with nothing but a rudimentary understanding of how to say "hello" and "thank you," letting it collect dust on their shelves as their lives become full with other projects. The solution is to try things for free (or very cheaply) *before* committing to a full purchase. For foreign language, check out free resources online or download an inexpensive app that will teach you the basics. For the gym, look for a free trial or guest pass option. If you still feel committed afterwards, go for the full purchase.

To Celebrate. Birthdays, promotions, accomplishments... they're all reasons to celebrate, and usually that entails spending money. I'm all for celebrating, but, personally, I know that I need to monitor how often I do it. 5 p.m. happy hour is *not* a reason to celebrate (as much as I'd like it to be).

To Be Social. Between your coworkers inviting you out for a cocktail and your twenty best friends inviting you to their engagement party, wedding shower, bachelorette party, and wedding, there is so much peer pressure to spend. I adore my friends and all of our social gatherings, but I simply don't have enough money to do it all and still prioritize my *own* goals. To help combat social spending, I've started picking and choosing which events I attend, cutting back where I can (I wear the same dress to almost every wedding), and recommending cheaper alternatives (potluck anyone?).

To Reward. This is one I personally struggled with, especially when training for my first marathon. The months of preparation, in addition to the race itself, were difficult and painful—leaving me in a state of constant, self-justified "deservedness." Whenever I wanted a treat—be it food, new workout wear, or a night out to decompress—

I'd think to myself, "I deserve this." But the fact is, there's *always* a reason to "deserve" something. Life is tough, and coming home and grabbing a glass of wine after a hard day of work feels amazing. But those kinds of habits not only carry damaging health consequences, but they have serious financial implications as well.

Retail Seduction, Impulse Buys, and Upsells

Despite your best attempts to bring mindfulness to your spending, retailers know how to tempt you into opening your wallet—from enticing window displays to lure you into their store, to the bins of goodies near the cash register to get you spending even more.

Case Study: Retail Seduction

Right around Mother's Day, I was leisurely walking around the city on my lunch break, keeping my eyes peeled just in case I came across the perfect gift. Being on 5th Avenue in Manhattan, I knew that I was out of my price range, so I headed eastward along 23rd street, home to my favorite stretch of NYC thrift stores.

I went from massive ten foot window displays showcasing a few watches, to cluttered racks and shelves crowded with crap just a few streets over. As I was sifting through a pile of used and discarded home goods at Goodwill, I started thinking about how all of these items were at one time purchased. I imagined how they were originally displayed—shiny and new. Everything I picked up in the back corner of the store I could see in my mind's eye at Target or Pier 1, tempting me to put it in my basket and make the purchase. But as I rifled through the dust ridden bins, that temptation was noticeably absent.

Everything seemed to be in working condition. Sure, items weren't in their original packaging, but there were certainly no visible faults or defects. So if the items were the same, why the lack of temptation?

Am I really *that* easily manipulated by the in-store atmosphere and the glamour of the shopping experience? Why were the designer handbags on a dimly lit shelf behind the cash register at the thrift store not calling to me like the Coach bag so perfectly placed in the display on 5th Avenue? And conversely, why does a trip to Pier 1 make me feel like I *need* throw pillows, when I don't give them a second look otherwise?

I accompanied a good friend of mine on a trip to Anthropologie one day when we were each shopping for wedding gifts. I don't shop in the traditional sense very often, so I remember feeling overwhelmed when I walked in the store. It was all *so beautiful.* I kept thinking, I want all of this! There were even moments of, "I don't even know what this is, but I want it!"

But then I thought, why should I buy a twenty dollar coaster from Anthropologie when I can get an equally awesome one for a buck or two at the thrift shop? Hello, lifestyle inflation!

After this thrift shop epiphany, I challenged myself to remain hyperaware in any retail environment. I now ask myself, "Do I really *need* this? Do I even *want* this? Or am I just being seduced by a well-crafted retail atmosphere? Is this purchase going to serve me or will it just take up space in my apartment until it eventually winds up in the back corner of the local Goodwill?"

Case Study: Avoiding an Impulse Buy

I found myself in Lululemon one day on my way home from work—always a dangerous place for me and my wallet. After picking up three items on the clearance rack, I wound up with two additional pieces in hand by the time I reached the dressing room.

Luckily, three of the items didn't fit as I had hoped. The other two items, neither of which were on sale, were similar enough that I was able to talk my way down to one. I wrestled with that last item though. Adorable pink shorts, perfect for my summer time marathon training, complete with moisture wicking material and zip pockets for storage. Oh so hard to resist.

Somehow my willpower pulled through and I managed to part the store without making a single purchase. It was hard to walk away, but honestly, thinking rationally in retrospect, it would've been even harder to part with fifty-four bucks—FOR SHORTS!

I thought to myself, "I'm really okay without them. I was okay without them before I knew they existed and I'll be okay without them in the future." But just in case I have a sudden undeniable *need* for high performance shorts, I snapped a quick picture on my phone with all the details. Who knows, maybe I'll find them on eBay.

Instituting a plan for impulse buy temptations—be it snapping a picture of the item to look up later or simply waiting twenty-four hours before deciding whether the purchase is really worth it—can make the difference between a conscious spending choice and blowing an entire paycheck on unnecessary items.

Case Study: Avoiding the Upsell

I was once the target of upselling twice within a span of ten minutes. The first encounter was at the Aveda salon. They were advertising student haircuts for twelve dollars. When I went inside to book an appointment, they offered me the choice of upgrading to a fourth-year student stylist for eighteen dollars, *just* six dollars more.

Minutes later I left the salon and went to the movies. I had a coupon for a free small popcorn. During redemption, the cashier offered me an upgrade to a medium for just fifty cents more. Sure, it's *just* another fifty cents...or it's *just* another six dollars, but do I really *need* the upgrade?

I used to always fall victim to the upsell. After all, what's another small percentage increase if I'm already paying X dollars? But on the other hand, I didn't even finish my small popcorn, so what's the point of paying an extra fifty cents if it's going to waste? And my twelve dollar haircut suited me just fine. Better than fine, in fact.

When you're standing at the cash register faced with a split-second decision, the pressure is on and retailers know it. In fact, they're banking on it—literally. Feel free to step away for a moment so that you can take time to think through your options rationally.

Cost vs. Labor—The Ultimate Reality Check

To help take the emotions out of spending and get immediately grounded in reality, I use the *cost vs. labor value assessment.* This simple strategy values the cost of an item by how many hours of work would be required to purchase it. Sometimes, it's incredibly disheartening (ahem, rent payments). But it's a valuable way to measure whether a contemplated purchase is worthwhile.

Assume your average hourly income after taxes is $15, now let's play cost vs. labor…

- Two weeks of groceries: $120 = 8 hours labor
- Happy hour drinks (with tip): $6 = 24 minutes labor
- Monthly MetroCard: $113 = 7 hours 30 minutes labor
- Grande Mocha at Starbucks: $5 = 20 minutes labor
- Dining out with friends (with tip): $25 = 1 hour 40 minutes labor
- Lululemon jacket: $108 = 7 hours 12 minutes labor

Does looking at your purchases this way make you re-think any of *your* spending choices?

Price Check: Know Before You Go

I love that when I go to Chipotle and order a burrito, I know that it's going to cost around eight dollars. Maybe a little more with New York City prices, maybe a little less in a small Midwestern town, but all in all, I know that eight dollars is standard. What I also know is that if my bill is significantly *more* than eight dollars, something is off and needs to be fixed.

Unfortunately, not everything in life is as transparent and defined as the cost of a Chipotle burrito. For instance, when I go to an auto body shop, how am I supposed to know when a price quote should raise a red flag? Even with some research, there are so many variables—location, service, parts needed—that I don't know how to begin calculating a standard fair price.

Among skilled service businesses—mechanics, plumbers, tailors, cobblers, etc.—price lists are practically non-existent. As much as I'd love to trust my local business owner not to grossly overcharge me or take advantage of my ignorance, experience has taught me otherwise. And while I always appreciate a recommendation from a friend, who's to say they haven't been ripped off, too?

While I've come to approach all services with a critical eye, I wonder what percentage of consumers accept pricing for what it is, without hesitation. Consider how many hundreds (or thousands) of dollars you could save over the course of your lifetime simply by questioning prices that seem out of line. While you can never be entirely sure that you're receiving a fair price, here's what you can do to reduce the risk of being overcharged.

Ask the Experts. Reach out to people who have experience in the field of your query to get their expert opinion on what kind of prices you should expect to pay for the services that you require.

Read Reviews. Not only do you want a good price, but you deserve good quality, too. For the best value, read online reviews (1-star, 5-star, and some in between). This also gives you an opportunity to do additional price comparisons before settling on a certain business or service provider.

Do Research. A simple Google search for "fair or standard price of ____" is a great place to start.

Ask Questions. Don't hesitate to ask about unexpected fees or price inflations on your bill (which you should always check thoroughly before paying).

Negotiate

Sometimes, getting the deal that you want or the price that you need requires a bit of negotiation. It's not just limited to the service industry, either. More things are negotiable than you might think, including cable bills, credit card rates, gym memberships, salaries, medical bills, and rent, to name a few.

To negotiate successfully, follow these basic guidelines:

Ask for What You Want. Be kind, direct, clear, and articulate. They can always say "no," but they might say "yes."

Be Prepared to Walk Away. You probably won't get exactly what you want—hence the term "negotiating"—but know ahead of time what price is your deal breaker.

Lay Your Cards on the Table. If you're not getting the quality you deserve for the price that you're paying, let the other party know that you'll need to cancel your membership, find a new bank, etc. If they still don't budge on price, you can confidently leave knowing that you've exhausted all of your options. If they *do* decide to come around, then congrats, you've successfully negotiated.

Once you've negotiated a price or settled on an item or service that you feel provides value, double check your bill and receipt. Part of conscious spending happens after the fact, when you ensure that you've been charged the agreed upon price for the goods or services received.

Don't Pay for the Mistakes of Others

The amount of mistakes made on everything from small daily purchases to weekly paychecks is astounding. No one has better intentions for your money than you. Retailers only stand to gain from a mistaken overcharge. If you don't care enough to check your receipts and rectify mistakes, you're the one who loses.

Case Study: Restaurant Mistake

One night my girlfriends and I went out to celebrate a very special birthday. I knew I'd be splurging a bit so I checked the menu online before heading out. I wanted to have an idea of how much I'd be spending. I settled on a moderately priced mushroom ravioli, but when I arrived at the restaurant, the price was 20 percent more than the price listed online.

Sure, in the scheme of things it was only an additional three dollars, but then I got to thinking—if everyone's dish cost 20 percent more, that would be a substantial dollar amount difference—especially with a party of ten. I pulled up the restaurant's website on my phone and pointed out the discrepancy to the manager. We wound up with a table full of complimentary desserts that night.

The point isn't that we scored free dessert, but that I spoke up when I noticed a mistake. While I've enjoyed refunds, free replacements, complimentary gift cards, and in this case, free dessert, I only speak up if I feel there's a legitimate complaint to be made. I don't seek to take advantage of a business, but I also don't want a business to take advantage of me, even unintentionally. Over the years I've learned that silence isn't always golden and it's worthwhile to point out mistakes and ask for what I deserve—100 percent satisfaction.

Case Study: Credit Card Error

In a span of six months, I found five errors on my credit card bill. Not only that, but after calling the companies that overcharged me, I had to follow up with two of them yet again to get the errors fixed. It happens all the time on purchases of all sizes. I once made a $1,000 purchase on my credit card and was accidentally charged twice. Can you imagine losing $1,000 just because you didn't double check your credit card statement?

You may be thinking, "Well, I'd notice a $1,000 difference!" But you may not notice five or ten dollars, and those small errors can add up fast. More importantly, by immediately reporting a ten dollar charge that you didn't authorize, you may be preventing more fraudulent charges in the future.

Unfortunately, these kinds of mistakes are not limited to retailers and credit card companies. Mistakes are often made on the income side, too. For this reason, it's important that you double check your pay stub *each week.* Make sure that all of your hours, including overtime, have been accurately accounted for, and speak up if you notice an error.

Case Study: Paycheck Mistake

Not too long ago, I had a payment incident with my employer. I was having fifty dollars deducted from my paycheck each week to pay off my union membership initiation fee. The day I paid off my membership, I contacted both the union and my employer to make sure that the fifty dollars would not be deducted from future paychecks. Lo and behold, the next week fifty dollars was deducted, despite taking every precaution.

The lesson? Don't assume anything is or will be taken care of—even if you've carefully covered all of your bases. Your paycheck is just one of hundreds or thousands to your employer, but to you, it's your livelihood. If you want to receive all of the money you're entitled to, it's up to *you* to keep track of it.

Track Everything

If you're willing to do one thing today to start improving your finances and preparing for your financial future, do this—*track everything.*

Writing down every penny earned and spent is the ultimate practice of *financial mindfulness.* When you know exactly how much you're earning, you have a definitive amount available to budget and to spend. With a detailed record of your spending laid out in front of you, you can focus entirely on the numbers. Without the emotions of the purchasing process affecting your judgment, you can objectively assess where you can cut back and save.

Use a spreadsheet, an app on your phone like Spending Tracker or Mint, fancy financial software like Quicken, or the back of a napkin to begin tracking. As long as it's all in one place, you'll be able to get a clear picture of your income and expenses, and a better understanding of your overall spending habits.

Make a Plan

How much do you want to save this year? Divide that number by twelve, and that's how much you have to save each month. Once you've tracked your spending, you can decide where the money will come from to meet your savings goal. If it helps, break down the numbers even further. Divide them into weeks or even days. Saving an extra $3,000 per year may sound daunting, but when it's broken down to $8.22 per day, it's a number that becomes more manageable. Packing lunch and cutting back on a few "latte factors." Done.

Sure, it might not be this simple. You can take the time to write out the perfect plan, but unless you put it into action on a daily basis, it won't do you any good. Beware of "habit sabotage"—the daily purchases that you make just because they're the purchases that you've always made in the past. Things like coffee and lunch on-the-go are probably the most common, but others like snacks, cigarettes, and bottled water are common saboteurs, too.

If you come across a recurring expenditure while tracking your spending, see if there's a way that you can eliminate it, replace it, or reduce its cost. Know exactly what new habits or routines you need to establish to make those changes easier. For example, if lunch on-the-go is eating up ten dollars per day, get in the habit of waking up fifteen minutes earlier to pack lunch instead. Or if happy hour is becoming a regular budget buster, schedule dinnertime potlucks. Learn to replace old habits with new frugal lifestyle choices so that you don't default to old patterns of spending. Instead, when you *do* decide to splurge on the occasional workday lunch or happy hour celebration, it will be a consciously planned spending decision.

The Cost of Procrastinating

Planning in general, from big picture budgeting to day-to-day living, is an integral part of conscious spending. If you have a tendency to procrastinate, you might be paying for it, quite literally…

Commuting. Running late can lead to a significantly more expensive commute. For me, as a New Yorker, it typically comes down to taking the subway or hailing a cab—that's a choice between spending three dollars on mass transit and at least ten dollars on a taxi. Needless to say, I always leave enough time to catch the train, or better yet, ride my bike.

Meals. Failing to pack lunch, bring snacks, and plan dinners at home can lead to an expensive grab-and-go habit. Dropping into the local deli or visiting the office vending machine for an afternoon pick-me-up carries a convenience cost that can add up quickly when it becomes a daily habit. There's no need to cut out afternoon snacking. Just buy in bulk and bring from home instead. Or, if you have trouble remembering to pack a daily snack, bring the whole box and keep it at your desk!

Travel. You may get lucky and find a last minute deal, but generally speaking, booking travel at the eleventh hour is an expensive endeavor. According to *International Business Times*, "...the worst time to buy a [plane] ticket is the day before. Two days before is a close second, and then three days, and so on..." You probably have to request your vacation days or confirm visits with family and friends in advance anyway, so make your travel arrangements as soon as possible to avoid getting stuck with an expensive last minute booking.

Expedited Services. From shipping a package to dropping off dry cleaning, a quick turnaround will cost you. I recently renewed my passport and know firsthand that expedited service costs *an additional sixty dollars* plus the cost of overnight delivery. Note expiration dates on all important documents and service contracts. Mark your calendar with special events that require specific preparations. Then flip your calendar to a week and a month before and make a note to deal with each of these items and expirations ahead of time.

Seasonal Purchases. From clothing to holiday decorations, the best deals are always available at the end of each season. Rather than stocking up on winter boots in March, and Christmas decorations in January, the majority of consumers continue to pay a premium for shopping during peak price season. Shop smarter by planning ahead and taking advantage of end of season clearance deals.

"Drop In" Buys. A quick trip to the drugstore to buy shampoo, deodorant, or whatever you just ran out of is almost always more expensive than planning ahead by purchasing in bulk, using coupons, or ordering online. When it comes to dry goods, paper products, personal care, and other non-perishables that you consistently use, stock up when you see savings or order online when you find yourself running low.

When you put off necessary purchases and errands until the last minute, you give up your power to be a savvy shopper. Without the luxury of time to thoroughly assess value, search for discounts, and comparison shop, the short-term objective of getting what you need trumps long-term savings and utility.

Plan for the Irregular

Sometimes we fall short of planning sufficiently because we fail to consider an expense or an entire category of expenses altogether. Housing, utilities, groceries, transportation, cell phone bill, etc.—those good old-fashioned budget categories are typically consistent from month to month, making them easy to plan for and budget. However, things like emergency room visits and unexpected car repairs are among the unanticipated, yet inevitable, events for which we need to store extra money in our savings accounts. Then there are the big-ticket purchases that range from laptops to vacations, for which we need to save our precious pennies for months ahead of time.

Even with a financial plan in place that considers all of these contingencies, there is one category that consistently takes me by surprise and threatens to disrupt my carefully allocated funds. I haven't figured out a good name for it, but it's something along the lines of "Oh crap, yeah *that* thing," although I guess we could be boring and call it "irregular expenses" or "miscellaneous." These kinds of expenses are characterized by the fact that they are typically recurring, even expected, but inconsistent and, therefore, sometimes surprising.

For instance, my once-every-ten-year passport renewal cost $110. I can say, "Oh well, it will all even out next month. At least I won't have to pay that for another ten years!" But the fact is, something like this seems to come up just about every month, and sometimes several at the same time. To prevent further "surprises," I added a miscellaneous category to my budget for things like passport renewals, car registration, license fees, and so on. It provides a buffer so that I don't need to tap my emergency fund or sacrifice my other savings goals when these costs arise. If I don't use all of the miscellaneous expense money in a given month, I'm sure the excess will get used shortly thereafter.

The main difference between an irregular expense and an emergency expense is that you can *predict* and *plan* for the irregular, whereas the *specific need* for an emergency fund is unknown ahead of time. For example, the renewal of your contact lens order or your vehicle registration is infrequent, but it's something that you know to anticipate—whereas an unexpected layoff or medical incident qualifies as an emergency.

Just as we prepare our finances for emergencies, we need to do the same with irregular and inconsistent expenses. Start by listing all of your irregular expenses, such as insurance payments, medical check-ups, estimated taxes, renewals, special occasions, gifts, etc. Then estimate your total annual cost for these expenses and divide by twelve to determine how much you need to budget for each month. Considering how forgetful we are when it comes to these types of expenses, add a 10 to 20 percent cushion to your budget.

Admittedly, there are times when the line between irregular and emergency expenses gets blurred. For instance, you may set aside cash for medical check-ups throughout the year, but if a follow up or two is required, you may find yourself crossing over into the e-fund. Home repairs can be similar—you set aside cash for regular maintenance and upkeep, but a major fix might require quite a bit more than your irregular expense buffer. In these situations, it's important to assess whether it's worth crossing the line from irregular expense to emergency fund. In the case of a medical problem, it very well may be. In the case of a home repair, it depends. Will you lose money or forgo safety by not fixing the problem right away? If yes, then it's an emergency fund fix—if not, you may want to hold off until you've saved enough in your budget to fund the repair. Remember that temporary inconvenience is a small price to pay for keeping your emergency fund intact. If you *do* drain your emergency fund to cover irregular expenses, you leave yourself exposed to *actual* emergencies.

Contingency Budgeting

Just as you plan for the unexpected by maintaining an emergency fund, you can also prepare by creating an *emergency budget*—a specific plan for how you would pay your bills if you suddenly lost your income or had to fund a medical emergency. This is what we'll call the "low budget."

To figure out your low budget, strip away as many of your expenses as possible and limit your costs to the bare-bones necessities. Don't think long term, just ask yourself, what can I live without for *one month*?

It's amazing how many of the expenses we've come to think of as "necessary" fall away when we only consider sacrificing them for a short period of time. Our habits and justifications for spending become so rooted within us that we forget that we *chose* them and that other options are available. The low budget is about breaking those habits and putting new, constructive ones in place.

Once you've identified the cost of your true necessities (housing, transportation, food), you'll know how much income you need to bring in *at a minimum*. If you're not hitting that minimum, even with your low budget, you need to either take on a second job, ask for a raise, or find ways to reduce the cost of your necessities.

Another contingency to plan for is an unexpected windfall of cash—a new job, a promotion, an inheritance, a big payout, etc. This will be your "high budget." Not only is your high budget useful in preparing for future cash flow increases, but it's also a fun exercise for bringing clarity to your goals and dreams. When you identify how you would use your increased cash flow, you begin to create that rich reality for yourself—it's a positive affirmation in action. If you don't have a reason to spend money, you won't have a reason to earn it. Think of your high budget as your financial dream board. Those dreams will become your reasons to continue saving.

Notice that the word "budget" never goes away, regardless of low or high income levels. Even luxurious expenses and splurges require a plan to ensure that spending never exceeds income. Excess cash without a plan or purpose disappears. If you get in the habit of spending more than you earn, you'll always be on the verge of going broke, regardless of your income. The key to long-term financial solvency and sustainable wealth lies in the simple practice of *conscious spending.*

Living a Fiscally Responsible Life

I've found that learning to live a fiscally responsible life is a lot like learning to live a healthy life. Crash dieting doesn't work and neither do get rich quick schemes. What *does* work is a total lifestyle change. In dieting, it's learning to develop a health conscious mindset and implementing that mindset in the form of healthy eating and exercise; allowing yourself the occasional piece of cake or pint of beer, but only in moderation. The same goes for spending. You must develop a mindset that defines your true necessities, keeping your spending in line with what is actually needed and valued. Temporary splurges like going out to eat and nights on the town should only be in moderation.

Cleanse Your Spending

To help kick start your new healthy spending lifestyle, try challenging yourself with a "spending cleanse." You can structure your spending cleanse however you like. You can go cold turkey and commit to zero spending for as many consecutive days as possible (though you may want to wait until you have a fully stocked fridge), or you can adopt a more moderate approach and simply eliminate discretionary, nonessential spending on items like movies, clothes, and alcohol. Lastly, you can cleanse by setting reduced spending limits for certain, problematic budget categories, or eliminate those categories altogether

Set Your Time Frame

If you're avoiding spending altogether, you may need to limit your cleanse to only a few days. But if you're trying to stick to reduced budget limits or eliminate discretionary spending, see if you can extend your cleanse for a month or two. For vice-only cleanses, you might challenge yourself to continue cleansing forever (especially if you're targeting an expense like cigarettes or soda that may be harmful to you in other ways).

Avoid Temptation

I typically use my credit card to rack up reward points, but when I'm on a spending cleanse I prefer to stick to cash so that I can't spend more than my designated withdrawal limit. Cash is tangible. Parting with the physical entity makes spending more grounded in reality. I can also see how much I have left at any moment and assess the value of a given purchase against how much cash I have in hand.

A spending cleanse not only generates more savings, but it helps foster financial mindfulness by targeting habitual spending and breaking bad money patterns. A spending cleanse is a concrete exercise for adjusting your money mentality, redefining your necessities, and freeing up cash to devote towards larger savings goals.

Another tactic for cutting back is to find alternative, more affordable ways to approach expenses—everything from essential spending to discretionary indulgences is up for adjustment. This practice is known as *frugality*.

CHAPTER 5

---•---

Frugal is Fabulous

For some reason, the word "frugal" carries an unwarranted negative connotation. Just as money is an unnecessarily taboo talking point, being thrifty, economical, or the "f-word" is something that people don't like to be called or associated with. I can't tell you how many eye rolls I've encountered in response to my hesitancy to shell out cash for overpriced dinners, parties, and getaways. But despite the occasional snide remark, there are some perks to being known as the "frugal one."

I Get the Old and Unwanted Things. This doesn't sound nearly as awesome as it is. Let me explain. When people have amazing outfits that don't fit them correctly, or purses they never end up using, or furniture they want to give away, I'm the first person they think of. They know how much I love freebies, so naturally they call me.

I'm the Deal Hoarder. Honestly, who doesn't love a good deal? When you're known as the "deal finder," everyone wants to tell you about the deal they just read about or claimed. I only have so much time to research the latest bargains myself, but with all the extra info that I receive from family and friends, my reach grows exponentially.

I Get the Offers. Lots of folks would like to cash in on easy extra income generators like babysitting, personal assisting, or other part-time and one-time jobs, but being known as the "income opportunist," I always get the offers first.

While I'm admittedly passionate, sometimes to a fault, about saving money, I'm never an advocate for being *cheap.* Frugality and cheapness are both practices aimed at saving money, but there is a fine line between the two.

Frugal people will not save money at the expense of others.

When dining out with a group of friends, I suggest that everyone pay for their own order and calculate their individual tax and tip rather than splitting the bill evenly, but I would never dream of leaving less than an 18 percent tip on my tab, unless the service was abysmal. I might skip the drink order and stick to an appetizer to reduce my bill, but saving money at the expense of the wait staff or my other friends by failing to account for taxes or "forgetting" to leave a tip would just be cheap.

Cheapness uses price as a bottom line; frugality uses value as a bottom line.

Clothing is one of those items where cheapness really shows itself. I love a fun five dollar shirt from H&M just as much as the next girl, but I'm not going to use it as a wardrobe staple. I'd much rather invest in more expensive, quality clothing pieces that will hold up over time, providing a better value in the long run.

Cheap people are driven by saving money regardless of the cost; frugal people are driven by maximizing total value, including the value of their time.

TLC's reality TV show *Extreme Cheapskates* is the best example of cheap versus frugal that I've ever seen. In one episode, a man spends several hours searching for change inside his home and around town. By the end of his search, he's come up with over seven dollars, which is admittedly impressive, but begs the question, "Is your time really worth less than seven dollars an hour?"

Being cheap is about spending less; being frugal is about prioritizing your spending so that you can have more of the things you care about.

I stick to ordering water at restaurants, I make my coffee at home, and I opt for running year-round rather than paying for a gym membership. I find small savings strategies in my day-to-day life so that I can allocate my resources to bigger dreams—my career in theatre, retirement, and travel, to name a few.

Those who are cheap are often afraid to spend money. They are willing to sacrifice quality, value, and time in order to cash in on short-term savings. Those who are frugal are resourceful with their spending, maximizing their dollars so they can fund big picture wants and dreams.

Frugal Can Be Fun

The other common misconception of frugality is that it's prohibitive to having fun. In my experience, though, I've found the opposite to be true. Not only is frugality a smart practice for prioritizing spending, but it has fostered innovation, critical thinking, and creativity, too. If anything, my frugality has opened more doors and opportunities than I ever thought possible.

Frugality is never about what you *can't* do, it's about learning and loving what you *can*; finding the freebies, the savings, and the strategies to live fabulously in the present while simultaneously planning for the future.

What's Keeping *You* from Being Frugal?

The resources for saving and information on the best deals are easily accessible to anyone capable of a simple web search. And yet, shoppers often fail to maximize their savings and select the best value options. If you find that you're consistently paying full price and missing out on simple savings, perhaps it's time to ask, what's keeping you from being frugal?

Old Habits. If you've shopped for clothes, groceries, or toiletries the same way for years, you've likely developed a method. The mere suggestion of a change in brand, be it toilet paper or sugar, might make you feel uneasy.

From the time of day that you shop to the way you organize your shopping cart, there's a great deal of habit and routine involved in the purchase process. While knowing what you want and how to get in and out of the store as quickly as possible is great for expediting the process, it's not necessarily the best financial choice. Being overly committed to a certain brand or store can keep you from seeing deals, specials, and alternate products that might provide a better value.

Even the savviest shoppers can miss out on savings opportunities if they remain too entrenched in their methods of searching for deals. Just think of how couponing has evolved since the early 1990s. If you never adapted to the online world, or more recently, the smartphone and app era, think of all the savings strategies you'd be missing.

Limited Time. Constraints on time leave less room for research, comparison shopping, and bargain hunting. If you wait until the last minute or find yourself rushing, you're more likely to purchase the item that you're most familiar with, rather than getting all of the information you need to make the best value assessment.

Tools like smartphone savings apps are a convenient way to save money while saving time. From comparing gas prices with GasBuddy to checking grocery costs with MyGroceryDeals, savings apps aggregate information in the palm of your hand so that you can search for deals and comparison shop on the spot.

Limited Energy. When you're exhausted after a long day or struggling to keep your kids from tearing apart the store racks, your lack of energy will likely have you searching for an exit strategy rather than a deal. Shopping on your own time, if you have that luxury, is best for bargain hunting.

Limited Information. Overspending stems from a lack of information or simply not knowing any better. Research helps, as does spending time improving your financial education. Keeping your financial literacy skills sharp and up to date provides you with a context and understanding of what constitutes a good deal. For example, knowing a bit about current interest rates and financing options will help you shop for an auto loan or negotiate with a car dealership or bank.

Information Overload. As helpful as it is to have as much information as possible, information overload can lead to purchase paralysis—the inability to make a purchase for fear of not getting the best possible deal. For example, if you've thoroughly researched the average price of cross-country flights and checked all of the discount airlines and aggregate flight sites on a daily basis, you might find yourself holding off again and again, anticipating a price drop or a new piece of information that will lead to a better deal. The inability to go ahead and pull the trigger may cause to you miss the window of opportunity on securing the best price.

Limited Resources. Sometimes you have to spend money to save money. For example, when shopping for a home, the higher your down payment, the less you'll have to pay in interest over the life of your mortgage.

Justifications. Our own justifications and excuses are often the biggest culprits of savvy shopping sabotage. Phrases like "I need," "I deserve," and "yeah, but..." should raise a red flag, even if you're only thinking them! These are all ways to justify spending, and if you have to justify it, it's probably not the best buy. Of course, the occasional splurge here and there is understandable, but consistent justification of splurges can lead to a consistent pattern of poor spending.

Fostering Frugality: Start Small

The easiest way to start implementing frugal lifestyle choices is to start small with day-to-day habits. Setting a precedent for savings with your most basic life tasks can help develop your frugal mindset so that you can save on larger purchases and make better value judgments in the future. Think of it as fiscal hygiene—preserving your financial wellness through daily maintenance and upkeep. Here are some examples of day-to-day actions that foster frugality and secure savings in the long run.

Exercise. According to the World Health Organization, physically active people save about $500 annually in healthcare expenses. Get your heart pumping to boost your immune system and reduce your risk of cancer, diabetes, and heart disease. Prevention pays.

Cook. Stop paying for convenience and cook your own food! It's not a dangerous or highly specialized skill. You are entirely capable of doing it, even if your go-to excuse is "I burn toast." Start simple with sandwiches and salads, or toss everything into a pan for a quick and easy stir-fry. Planning your meals and eating at home will easily trim your food costs, and, if done properly, your waistline.

Floss. It wasn't until I had to spend $250 on a tooth extraction and another $1,800 on a dental implant that I became a daily flosser. Those numbers are real, and I'm not going to part with another $2,000 just because I didn't take that extra minute each day to floss. Do yourself a favor, start flossing now and save yourself the cost *and pain* of cavities, root canals, extractions, implants, crowns, and gum disease.

Use Public Resources. Free public resources like libraries are shockingly underutilized in favor of more expensive alternatives. Did you know that public libraries often loan CDs, DVDs, periodicals, musical scores, and eBooks to their members? Before signing in to iTunes to purchase the latest season of *Game of Thrones* or download the latest bestseller onto your eReader, check your free local resources first.

Comparison Shop. What's your typical shopping behavior? Do you search for what you need, or do you put the first item in your line of vision into your cart? Do you always choose the same brands regardless of price? Do you buy whatever is on sale?

The sooner you get into the habit of questioning traditional retail pricing and your approach to it, the better. Take the time to research the best values, develop price comparison strategies, and learn to use money saving apps like RetailMeNot and PriceGrabber to their fullest capacity.

Track Your Finances. ATM fees, overdraft fees, late fees, interest payments… How much money could you save if you were more diligent about tracking your finances? Seeing *how* and *where* you spend money allows you to take a look at your financial footprint and pinpoint exactly where you can afford to cut back and save big.

Personal Savings Strategies

In addition to basic, universal savings strategies, you'll also need to develop personal tactics for day-to-day savings. If there's one thing I've learned, it's that personal finance is truly *personal.* We all have different ways of prioritizing and shaping our financial futures. With that in mind, review the tools and options provided and choose the strategies that work best for you.

Stock Up on Socks and Underwear. Spending time and money hauling your wardrobe to and from the laundromat should be avoided as much as possible. To make your wardrobe stretch, re-wear staples like jeans and jackets, and stock up on the items that you need to change every day like socks and underwear. With a full drawer dedicated to these essentials, you'll only have to do laundry once or twice each month.

Cut Back on Primping. I work in the entertainment industry so I appreciate the importance of appearance, but I'm not willing to spend sixty dollars every six weeks to get my hair trimmed and my roots done. Simple techniques like waiting an additional few weeks between haircuts or painting your own nails will save you hundreds of dollars on personal care costs each year.

No Pets. I can barely afford to pay my own rent, buy my own food, and pay for my own healthcare, let alone provide all of that for a pet. I also never want to be faced with the decision of treating a pet's expensive medical condition or letting the pet die. (I know this is a sensitive topic, so a gentle reminder—that's just *me,* pay for pet care if that's your priority.)

Netflix. The average cost of a movie ticket is twelve dollars, and seeing a 3D movie will set you back twenty dollars! Personally, I'd rather trade three movie nights for a chance to see a Broadway show. In the meantime, I'm a Netflix junkie. At less than ten dollars per month, with all of the amazing new content and instant accessibility, I'm happy to stay in.

Use Freebies. Always try to utilize freebies that are built into the price of a purchase. For instance, when I stay at a hotel, I pack up the complimentary shampoos and conditioners each night so that I will get new ones when they clean the room the next morning. Now I have a stockpile of practically new travel sized soaps for future camping trips and family visits.

Run. A membership to a sports club can cost upwards of eighty dollars per month. Consider enjoying a long *free* run instead.

Ditch the Party Lifestyle. Serial splurging on expensive club covers and fourteen dollar cocktails is not cool, sexy, or smart. I prefer to find ways to be social without committing budget suicide. Potlucks, free concerts and events, and the occasional happy hour are all great alternatives to overpriced restaurants, costly entertainment, and pricey drinks.

Learn. Everything that I know about saving and making money I learned at some point. Continuing to read and stay tuned in to the latest information is critical. If you know the fair price of an item, you won't allow yourself to be scammed. If you understand how to use your credit card effectively, you can earn cash back rather than pay interest. If you learn how to invest wisely, you can grow your money rather than lose it to inflation.

Pick and Choose. Recognize your indulgences like Starbucks and happy hour for what they are—indulgences. Make sure they don't become regular occurrences that interfere with your ability to create a secure financial future. Knowing that you can *choose* to make a purchase rather than mindlessly buying out of habit is a powerful lesson to learn.

Find Alternatives. For those things that you don't want to cut out of your lifestyle, but need to spend less on for the sake of your budget, look for alternative strategies and approaches. My core philosophy is that there's almost always a cheaper way of doing or buying the things that you want. If you make an effort to research what those alternatives are, you'll find continued savings in the future.

Let's explore some low-cost alternatives in more detail.

Alternative Savings Strategy: Rent

When we discuss the merits of renting versus buying, it's typically in the context of the housing market. But what if we took a more universal approach to assessing our rent versus buy options?

Thanks to the Internet, what can be rented has expanded to include almost everything. Whether you need occasional access to a vehicle or a specialized tool for a one-time project, be sure to consider your rental opportunities first.

Should You Rent, Lease, or Buy a Car?

While I generally don't recommend leasing a car, buying a new or used car isn't always the most cost effective alternative, particularly for those who live in big cities. When parking comes at a premium and public transit is readily accessible, short-term car rental on an as-needed basis can be significantly more cost effective than full-time car ownership. Here are some terrific rental options to consider.

Zipcar. Zipcar offers car rentals through a membership program. With the flexibility to rent by the hour or the day and many convenient locations nationwide, Zipcar is a cost-effective option for those who need occasional automobile access.

RelayRides/Getaround. RelayRides and Getaround facilitate person-to-person car rentals. Car owners post information about their vehicles along with availability and price. When the renter finds a vehicle that suits his or her needs, they can request a trip time. Once a mutual agreement is made, the renter picks up the car and returns it as planned. Both sites have a peer review system to rate renters and vehicle owners.

Lyft/Uber. Skip the rental altogether and opt for on-demand ridesharing with the touch of a button. Lyft and Uber are apps that allow passengers to connect with nearby drivers to get where they need to go.

Alternatively, if you own a car and can tolerate the risk of a stranger driving your vehicle or riding alongside you, then you can earn extra income with these apps and services, too.

Should You Rent or Buy a Bike?

As a city dweller, I prefer to use a bike as my primary mode of transportation, but I have yet to take the plunge and buy my own. I opt for my city bike sharing program, which saves me from worrying about storage, theft, maintenance, and traveling with a heavy lock and chain across town.

When I travel out of town, I prefer to scour Craigslist for bike rentals rather than the expensive, local retailers. One summer, while working in Burlington, Vermont, a coworker of mine decided to buy a cheap bike from Craigslist to get around town. At the end of the summer, she relisted the bike on Craigslist and managed to sell it for her original purchase price. Four week bike rental, absolutely free... Not a bad deal!

What about Equipment, Tools, and Everything Else?

Websites like Loanables.com and Zilok.com serve as online rental marketplaces for just about everything from Xboxes to sewing machines to ladders. Determining which items to rent and which to buy will depend on your specific needs and circumstances. For any item that you're considering, review these questions:

- What is your projected cost per use of the item? Will you use it enough to justify buying it?
- Are there any additional costs to consider such as maintenance, repair, time, and storage?
- Do you prefer the convenience of renting?
- Do you prefer the convenience of ownership?

The decision to rent or buy will differ from person to person and from item to item. One of my favorite examples to illustrate the subjective nature of the rent versus buy decision is formal wear.

Formal Wear: The Case to Buy

You Can Repurpose. Since I was sixteen years old, I've probably attended two or three formal events each year. And by formal, I mean black tie, full-length gown standard. In addition, I probably have another two or three cocktail dress occasions each year. Suffice it to say, having a few formal dresses on hand is a necessity in my life. If I were to rent a dress for each occasion, I would have paid for each of my gowns several times over by this point.

You Can Ensure Fit. When you buy your own dress, you can have it tailored to fit you like a glove, as opposed to a rental where you risk a length issue or a loose bodice.

Formal Wear: The Case to Rent

You're a Label Lover. As much as I repurpose my gowns, it would take *a lot* more wear to make a $4,000 designer label pay off. If you're a label lover, a dress rental company like Rent the Runway is a great option. Rentals typically cost between $40 and $250 for a four-day rental. To ensure fit, two sizes are shipped. When you're done, simply return the dress in a prepaid envelope and they take care of the rest.

Bridesmaids Dresses. Forget the dilemma of buying an expensive bridesmaid dress that you can never wear again. If you can rent the same dress, in sizes that work for each bridesmaid, then you can ensure quality fashion that fits your family and friends' budgets.

Temporary Weight Change. If you're in the middle of a temporary body transformation, be it pregnancy or an ongoing weight loss, a rental might be a good option for finding a dress that works for your current body type.

One-Time Occasion. I admittedly have an unusually high number of formal affairs to attend. If you're anticipating a one-and-done need for your formal outfit, you should consider renting. Unless, of course, you can buy and sell again when you're done.

Alternative Savings Strategy: Do It Yourself

Pinterest and reality television are leading the charge in the *Do It Yourself* savings trend. It's not just skilled craftsmen and professionals taking on tasks like carpentry, renovating, and decorating anymore. With the proper tools and enough time and inspiration from HGTV, anyone can participate in the D.I.Y. movement.

Cultivating a practical skill set, like learning to sew or do basic home repairs, can save you a great deal of money in the long run by eliminating your need to constantly hire help. There are, however, some cases in which certain tasks are best left to the pros. For complicated and intricate projects, the cost and frustration to D.I.Y. may not be worth the savings.

When Should You D.I.Y.?

A few months ago, my boyfriend and I were walking around one of the most dangerous places for an aimless shopper, The Container Store. You never knew how much you wanted or needed a storage unit until you've entered the masterful retail environment known as The Container Store.

As we were browsing, we played one of my favorite games, "Guess How Much This Costs." We walked by several pieces of furniture as we played the game, and while I scoffed at the retail values, my boyfriend seemed to think it was all very reasonable. I typically wouldn't rely on his assessment of what is and isn't affordable (he loves to spend money), but since he's a carpenter and we were looking at furniture, I wanted to understand his reasoning.

He explained that for him to buy the materials and build the pieces that we were assessing, it would cost more in the form of his *time* than it would to simply buy the completed piece of furniture. For instance, if a nicely styled, sanded, and stained small bookcase cost $100 at the store, and it would take over four hours to complete the same project at home, would it be worth his time if he typically gets paid over $25 per hour? Does a do-it-yourself project have to be less than your cost of labor to be worthwhile?

The answer is: It depends. In our furniture example, you'd have to consider the cost of materials and how long it would take to acquire them. A trip to Home Depot could be another hour of your time. You'd also have to consider if you have both the tools and space required to work on the project. Here in New York City, that can be tricky. Not to mention, if you work on the project elsewhere, you'll have to somehow transport it back to your apartment. (Furniture on the subway?) Suddenly, I'm understanding why D.I.Y. might not be the most attractive option all of the time.

However, if the D.I.Y. project you're considering is something that you enjoy doing, and you have the available time and resources to do it, then you might as well. There's nothing like a hobby that saves you money. But what if you have all of the resources and it's *not* something you particularly enjoy doing? If it *feels* like work, is it worth it then?

If you get paid $30 per hour at work, those hours are not only taxed, but they are finite. So even if the cost of labor on one D.I.Y. project comes out to only $25 per hour, it may still be worth pursuing since you're essentially capitalizing on hours that you could not profit from anyway.

Whether it's weighing your D.I.Y. options, comparing rental prices to ownership costs, or researching alternative approaches to your typical shopping behavior, fostering frugality is simply about taking a moment to stop and assess value before automatically engaging out of habit, peer pressure, or perceived necessity. By challenging yourself to maximize every dollar, you may find yourself stumbling upon fabulous opportunities and experiences that you never dreamed possible.

CHAPTER 6

———•◦•———

Beginner's Guide to Couponing

One of the central tenants of my frugal philosophy is getting more for less. The more affordable you can make your wants and needs, the more you can accommodate both larger financial goals and small day-to-day indulgences in your monthly budget. One of the best strategies to maximize this kind of affordability and "more for less" value is through couponing.

Step 1: Collect your coupons.

Coupons can come from anywhere—the Sunday paper, in-store circulars, in-store coupon machines, coupon books, online (Coupons.com, SmartSource.com), even from little peel-offs or "peelies" on the products themselves. The first step to becoming a savvy couponer is learning to spot coupons and collect them for later use.

Step 2: Get organized.

A pile of coupons won't do you any good. You need to know *exactly* what you have on hand and how to find each coupon quickly. You can use a binder or booklet and put stickers on the tabs to specify sections for different products. That way "spices and sauces" stay separate from "dairy and eggs"—when you have ten coupons this seems unnecessary, but when you have four hundred, you'll be grateful. Remember, *a coupon is only good if you can actually find it and use it.*

Step 3: Sign up for store savings cards.

Many major retailers only offer sale prices "with store card." *These are savings cards, not credit cards.* They are free at customer service counters, and they could mean the difference between paying five dollars or three dollars for an item.

Step 4: Know your coupons.

There are two types of coupons, manufacturer coupons (MQs) and store coupons (SQs). MQs are typically the coupons that come in the Sunday newspaper. They are for a specific product but not a specific store. SQs, on the other hand, are coupons that specific stores like Target and Walgreens release themselves.

Step 5: Use your coupons.

Once you've done the legwork—found the coupons, clipped, and organized them—how do you know the best time to use your coupons? Start by checking the circulars. Find out what's on sale. If you're in the area, take a quick walk around the store to see if anything exciting is on clearance (these sales tend not to be advertised). Then pull out your beautifully organized coupons and compare.

While saving $1.00 on a $3.50 can of soup is fine, you can do better. You want to find a store that has the product already on sale—in fact, as a rule, only use coupons on products that are already on sale. Perhaps the store also has an SQ, which reduces the price further. You can generally use an SQ and an MQ together—this is called "stacking," and it's the "perfect storm" of couponing.

To demonstrate the effect of coupon stacking, assume that you're shopping at CVS and you see a can of Progresso Soup marked down from $3.50 to $1.99, with store card. In the circular, there's an SQ for $1.00 off two cans, and you have two MQs for $1.00 off a single can. Here's the math for this transaction, assuming that you buy two cans:

- $3.50 x 2 cans = $7.00 (normally). Swipe your card, and they're magically reduced to $1.99 each.
- $1.99 x 2 cans = $3.98
- $3.98 – $1.00 (SQ) – $2.00 (both MQs) = $0.98 total or $0.49 each

That can of soup, which you might have purchased for $3.50 during your lunch break, now costs only $0.49—and you purchased two cans, saving $6.02 total (an 86 percent savings).

Do you have more coupons? Maybe buy four cans! Be smart, get only what you will use, or what you know people close to you will use, but do look beyond this week or this month. Will you eat soup eight times in the next six months? Great. Buy eight cans of soup.

A few words of caution…brand loyalty can be the death of a couponer. Say you like Garnier shampoo, but when you arrive at the store, you discover that you can buy L'Oreal shampoo for $0.75 cheaper. TRY IT. I have discovered amazing products this way.

Remember, each store is different, and it's the store's right to set their own coupon policy (or not accept coupons altogether). Don't expect your corner bodega to accept coupons—stick to the chain stores that have clear policies. If you can, pay a visit to the store's website in advance and print a copy of their coupon policy to carry with you while you shop.

Should You Try Couponing?

YES! Couponing takes a bit of legwork and effort to begin, but once you're up and running, it will turn into a well-oiled machine that's easy to maintain. Remember that coupons expire—usually in about a month—so go through your collection every few weeks and toss out the old ones. You'll learn there are many ways to avoid paying full price for something if you set your mind to it. When in doubt, visit TheKrazyCouponLady.com for advice—she is a couponing ninja. The most important lesson in couponing is to buy now, when it's cheap or free, so that you don't have to pay full price when you need it later.

Couponing for Non-Couponers

Confession: I actually *suck* at couponing, but I *love* to save money—bizarre combination, I know. I have no patience for searching through circulars and clipping coupons. On the other hand, I *hate* not getting the best deal possible, especially when the savings are significant and easy to be had. So I've been on the hunt for savings strategies that don't require the creation of a stockpile in my small NYC apartment, the constant cataloguing of coupons, or the stretching of my wallet with fifty different loyalty cards.

For Day-to-Day Savings...

While I lack the patience to do the whole *coupon-clipping thing*, I always take ten seconds to do a quick Google search for "[product name] promo code" before purchasing an item online or making a trip to the store. More often than not, I'm able to find some kind of savings, and most of the time that savings is in the form of a promo code on RetailMeNot.com.

When I finally upgraded to the modern world and got a smartphone, I downloaded the free RetailMeNot app. It now serves as my on-demand coupon service whenever I'm considering a purchase—from Seamless.com food delivery to picking up a new garlic press at Kmart.

I also recommend using price comparison apps like PriceGrabber and RedLaser in-store to make sure that you're paying the lowest price possible. A quick barcode scan will tell you if the product you're searching for can be purchased at a lower price at a nearby store.

For Indulgences...

As a food lover, life in the big city is like being on Temptation Island 24/7. There are so many amazing places to frequent on every corner and everywhere in between. I suffer from a combination of #FOMO (fear of missing out on unique delicacies) and anxiety of overpaying when I dine out. Luckily, I've found helpful apps and websites to ease the burden. LivingSocial, Groupon, Amazon Local, and Restaurant.com all make couponing simple with location-based deals. Depending on where I am when I'm craving my latest foodie indulgence, these services locate restaurants in the vicinity and offer on-demand savings and flash deal specials. While they're great for visiting my trusted favorites in my own neighborhood, they're also perfect for discovering new affordable restaurants when I'm out and about. And they're not just for food, either. I've found deals on everything from Broadway shows to booze cruises.

Are Deal Sites Always a Good Deal?

As much as I love using deal sites to find discounts at my favorite restaurants, entertainment venues, and travel destinations, there are legitimate reasons to be wary.

A while back, Groupon was offering a deal for $18 admission to the Metropolitan Museum of Art in New York City. When I came across it, over a thousand people had already bought in. Being a New Yorker, this so-called "deal" made me raise an eyebrow. While Groupon was advertising 28 percent off, I knew the *actual* price of admission was a $25 *suggested donation.* In other words, the price of admission to the MET is entirely up to you.

Consider this, according to NPR, deal sites like Groupon take *half* of total sales. So if your deal is half off, that means the retailer is only getting a quarter of the designated purchase price. In this case, the MET is getting $9 and Groupon is keeping the rest. So rather than spend $18 for a Groupon to the MET, simply go to the MET and donate $9 for your voluntary price of admission.

As much as I love to use services like Groupon, I've come to look at their "deals" with a critical eye. For an example like the MET, they're essentially employing a marketing tactic to create a discount where no real discount exists. If it attracts customers to the museum, that's excellent, but I'll be reserving my donation entirely for the museum itself. But I'm not writing off deal sites altogether. If purchased with a watchful eye, deal sites can open doors to experiences that you never thought were possible within your budget. To ensure that you enjoy the *good side* of Groupon, or any other deal aggregator, follow these essential guidelines.

Step 1: Read the fine print.

While you might casually skim or skip over the fine print on your iTunes agreement or the latest Terms and Conditions update from Twitter, the fine print on a Groupon may have a direct impact on whether or not you can actually use the deal being advertised. Be sure to consider all of the conditions that may present themselves in the fine print before purchasing the deal.

For example, you may be restricted to using your coupon on a specific date. If you're going to be out of town or have a prior commitment on that date, the deal isn't going to do you much good. Other types of restrictions can affect your experience. For example, many restaurant deals require you to order from a limited menu. A forty dollar dinner for two at the swankiest restaurant in town may sound like a steal, but not if the "Groupon menu" only offers pasta with garlic and olive oil.

In other cases, the fine print is accompanied by an asterisk, which usually indicates, in even tinier print, additional fees and charges that apply. Be sure that you know exactly what's included before making your purchase, especially if you're giving a Groupon as a gift. Similarly, be sure to review the refund and cancellation policy in advance. If you're on vacation and purchase a Groupon for a weather-dependent activity like whale watching, what is the policy if the event is cancelled? If you don't live in the area, you may not be able to reschedule, so make sure that you're permitted to a full refund.

Step 2: Research the business.

Get in the habit of researching the business that is offering the deal through Google or Yelp. You'd be amazed at how many of these businesses have received terrible reviews. (I've noticed this particularly with massages and spas.) You'll also be able to see what they regularly charge for the service you're considering. Perhaps they offer their own discount that is even cheaper than the Groupon price.

Step 3: Call the business.

You don't want to purchase a Groupon for a service that expires in three months only to find out there are no available appointments before that time. Some businesses overextend themselves when offering these deals. They become booked and suddenly you're stuck with an expired deal through no fault of your own. For this reason, I recommend calling the business *before* purchasing the Groupon to make sure you'll be able to use the deal.

Step 4: Negotiate.

While you're on the phone with the business, be sure to mention that you're considering purchasing their Groupon. Businesses will often allow you to book directly through them for the Groupon price, or they might even offer a better deal! Remember, when you purchase through Groupon the business only gets half of the already discounted price while Groupon collects the other half. You can use this knowledge to negotiate an even better deal with the business directly.

Are "Freebies" Always a Good Deal?

While you might be questioning the value of Groupons and other similar deals, how could something that's *free* possibly be a bad deal? While I wouldn't call freebies *bad*, I do think that it's smart to objectively consider whether they're always worth it.

There's admittedly something about the word "free" that creates excitement in my soul. I find myself bragging about things that I've gotten for free. When I receive a compliment on a piece of jewelry that I got from a friend who was cleaning out her closet, or a pair of pants that I picked up at a clothing exchange, I'm more eager to share that I got the item *for free* than I am happy about receiving the compliment. But lately, I've come to look at freebies with a more critical eye. I've learned that perhaps my excitement about receiving items for free has been clouding my judgment as to whether the freebie is truly worthwhile.

So how could something that's free not be worthwhile? After all, *it's free!* Bear with me as I review some of the costs associated with things that are "free."

Financial Cost. Freebies don't typically show up at your doorstep. There's probably some transportation cost involved and possibly more. For instance, if I have a friend who is giving away a mattress, I need to consider the cost of picking up that mattress and bringing it back to my apartment. Do I need to rent a car? Do I have to pay any tolls? Do I need to hire help? With all of these financial considerations, the mattress isn't exactly free anymore. And while those comparatively small expenses may be worthwhile for a mattress, they may not be worthwhile for something else like a cheap end table or used kitchen supplies.

Time Cost. How much time are you willing to trade for a freebie? Is it worth spending a weekend afternoon driving around the city to pick up a free mattress? Is it worth entering all of your personal information and signing up for a newsletter to receive a free sample product? Is it worth sitting through a timeshare presentation to get a free vacation? These considerations will vary from person to person, but they're definitely costs worth considering.

Health Cost. Ever been lured into an event or project with the words "free pizza" or "free beer?" I love free food and alcohol just as much as the next person, but is it worth spending an extra hour at the gym just to burn it off?

Physical Cost. Everything within your physical space, whether you received it for free or not, carries some kind of maintenance cost. Whether it's watering the plants given to you by your neighbor or dusting off the books given away down the block, you need to ask yourself whether the freebies are worth the time and effort it takes to maintain them.

Mental Cost. If you claimed all of the freebies that are available, you'd probably end up on an episode of *Hoarders.* Think critically about what you're getting and if it's worth the physical and mental clutter that it creates. I don't know about you, but I have better things to do with my physical, digital, and mental space than fill it with free t-shirts I'll never wear, free newsletters I'll never read, and free product samples I'll never use.

Practical Savings Strategies

In addition to the occasional worthwhile freebie or coupon, it pays to be equipped with practical savings strategies that can be used daily. The more you can reduce both necessary bills and discretionary spending, the more freedom you'll have to prioritize your money for short and long-term goals.

Be patient with yourself. Remember that your new "money diet" is just like any other diet. Putting new healthy habits in place is hard, frustrating, and can make you feel like giving up. Don't fall off the wagon! Even if you slip up and buy a new flat screen TV that you can't afford, one mistake doesn't have to throw you off course entirely. Go back to the basics and practice the small habits that foster frugality, then rebuild your financial confidence from there.

If you practice these strategies and follow through, you'll see results in the form of healthy, conscious spending habits that will stick with you for years to come.

CHAPTER 7

Practical Savings: Food

While microwaving Ramen Noodles might have been enough to get by in college, taking the time to develop your culinary skills will pay off in the long run. Eating prepared foods in the "real world" comes at a premium. One trip to the salad bar at Whole Foods will teach you that lesson real quick. Instead, find recipes online for the dishes that you love the most and learn how to prepare them at home. Start with one or two go-to meals that you can master and expand from there. Don't forget to make extra servings that you can take to work for tomorrow's lunch. It's time to start brown bagging again!

Get Excited about Eating In

When you get home after a long day, you just want to sit down, relax, and be served a nice meal. But if you're going to have any chance of breaking the auto dial delivery habit, you're going to have to get excited about eating in. Here are four suggestions to get started.

Pin It. If looking at pictures of food on Pinterest doesn't make you salivate with anticipation, I don't know what will. Pinterest is like an on-demand, customizable cookbook—and it's completely free. Just search for your favorite food or dish and find thousands of ways to prepare it.

If you don't know where to start, search "recipes" and then *favorite* or *re-pin* whatever catches your attention. (Uh oh, I was just doing this myself and found a copycat recipe of Auntie Anne's Cinnamon Sugar Pretzel Bites! Yum!)

Pinterest is also a great resource to help you figure out exactly what to do with that one ingredient that's beginning to go bad in your fridge. Search "_____ recipes" (for me, it's mushrooms) and go from "Ugh, I have to use these before they go bad" to "Woohoo, I can't wait to use these _____ (mushrooms)."

Try Some Add-Ins. Spice up your basic go-to dishes with some unexpected add-ins. I'm not talking about adding the same old grilled chicken to top off your bed of rice—get creative! I'm a fan of lentils and fresh spices in my salad, shredded zucchini and spaghetti squash mixed into my pasta, and avocado and spinach in my grilled cheese. These taste incredible and add a lot of nutritional punch to an otherwise bland meal.

Make Your Own Sauce. I've come to find that sauces and dressings can make or break a dish. One of the reasons food tastes so good at restaurants is because (most of the time) they make their own sauces.

The great thing about sauce is that you can make it in your spare time and then store it in your fridge to use when you want. The next time you get home after a long day and you're too exhausted to cook, grab some lettuce and your jar of homemade dressing, or heat up tortillas to smother with homemade enchilada sauce. You'll be amazed at what a difference the homemade sauce makes.

Make It an Event. Find a way to make dinnertime something that you look forward to—not just the eating part, but the prep time, too. You can make it an activity by inviting your spouse, your children, your roommate, or whomever you'd like to join you. You can make it social by hosting a potluck or inviting friends over for a meal that you can all make together. (Make your own quesadilla party? Topped with your homemade guacamole, of course.) Make it fun by putting on music and pouring a glass of wine to sip as you go. There are so many ways to bring joy and excitement into the kitchen. Once you find a method that works for you, I guarantee that you'll find yourself eating in more often.

Grocery Store Savings

Before you can begin cooking at home, you'll have to make it through the chore of grocery shopping. Without a savvy, in-store strategy, you can easily wind up spending more than you would at your favorite restaurant. Follow these grocery shopping guidelines to develop a routine of smart savings.

Know What You Already Have. Before going to the grocery store, take a quick inventory of your fridge and pantry. You don't want to wind up with three packages of expensive berries that spoil before you eat your way through them.

Make a List and Stick to It. Making a shopping list will help you stay focused on what you need, like whole grains, fruits, and veggies, instead of what you impulsively want, like a Snickers bar at the checkout counter.

Shop on a Full Stomach. Shopping when you're hungry can lead to poor decision making and overbuying. Grab a snack before hitting the store.

Compare Unit Prices. Just because a jar of peanut butter is twice the size of the one sitting next to it doesn't mean that it's a better value. Always make price comparisons based on the item's unit price (the price per pound, per ounce, etc.). Consider bringing a pocket calculator with you and allow yourself plenty of time at the store.

Buy Grains in Bulk. You'll find that the larger bags and bulk bins of brown rice generally have cheaper unit prices than the individual meal boxes. The same goes for the majority of your grains—barley, oats, cereals, etc. If you have the space, buy in bulk and store your grains in airtight containers to keep them fresh.

Buy in Season. When produce is in season, it's at its cheapest price and highest nutritional value. Try to plan snacks and meals that revolve around what's in season to get the best of both worlds.

Shop the Frozen Food Aisle. Buy bags of frozen produce—not the prepackaged, high sodium, frozen meals. For maximum health benefits and flavor, choose organic fruits and veggies. You'll save money by buying frozen.

Check Out Alternate Sources of Protein. Beans and lentils are excellent (and cheap) sources of protein that can be bought in bulk and stored for long periods of time. Try incorporating these powerhouse legumes into your meals on a regular basis to get major benefits while saving major bucks.

Buy Generic. When it comes to items that are of the same product quality, choose the generic over the more expensive name brand.

Buy Whole Foods. Oftentimes, the less processed that food is, the cheaper it is. For example, an apple is often cheaper than applesauce and dry beans are cheaper than their refried counterparts. A double win for you!

Shop the Perimeter of the Store First. Fill your cart with nutrient dense produce, protein, grains, and dairy, leaving less room for the processed junk food in the center of the store. Buying locally grown, organic products is ideal, but not always an option if your budget is tight. I do, however, recommend investing more of your grocery budget into fresh food. Remember that how food is grown has an impact on its quality, and consequently, your health. By buying organically grown foods, you reduce the potential health hazards posed by pesticides, additives, and genetically modified organisms (GMOs). An investment in your food now could save you money on medical bills later.

How to Save Money in the Kitchen

Every so often there's a notable stench in my apartment. I empty the garbage but the smell still lingers. I continue to look around for the culprit, but to no avail. Then I go to the fridge for a snack and it hits me, the smell of decay. I rifle through the shelves and bins to discover a bag of rotting spinach or a mushy cucumber.

You're probably all too familiar this situation. According to GreenBiz.com, the average American household spends $2,200 per year on wasted food! So how can we stop wasting food and money in the kitchen?

Reorganize Your Fridge. The fruit and vegetable drawers that come standard in most refrigerators seem like a bright idea, but in reality, they're a black hole for food—out of sight, out of mind. Don't keep the food that spoils the fastest hidden from view. I've spent too many evenings shuffling through my veggie drawer only to discover another soggy cucumber or dried-out citrus.

Take Inventory. I can't count the number of times that I've come home from the grocery store with cartons of veggie broth, only to find that I already had a full stash at home. While this is less of a problem with pantry items and non-perishables, milk and other quick spoilers don't hold up nearly as well. Keep a list of what you regularly use and make a note when items start running low.

Grow Your Own. Depending on where you live, you may not have room to grow a full garden, but I guarantee that you have room for one or two pots of fresh herbs. Grow your own basil, mint, oregano, and other favorite spices to add instant freshness to your dishes for a fraction of the cost.

Practice Portion Control. Not only will sticking to proper portion sizes help keep your waistline in check, but it will also make your food last longer. If you can cook once and eat twice (or more) for each of your meals, you'll also save on total energy use.

Be an Iron Chef. When you get down to the last few items in your fridge and they're nearing the end of their shelf life, rather than choosing one ingredient and throwing away the rest, think like an Iron Chef and fuse everything into one meal.

Skip the Specialized Appliances. Browsing the aisles of the department store kitchen section is a lesson in avoiding temptation. The waffle irons and ice cream makers practically sparkle under the lighting, tempting even the most practical shoppers with their novelty. But let's face it, there are only so many times that you're going to make use of that corn dog maker. Save the counter and cabinet space for necessities to keep your sanity and your wallet in check.

Keep Tupperware Organized. I used to be terrible about packaging my leftovers because my Tupperware drawer was a nightmare. Every time I opened it, some mismatched top or half-destroyed food container would fall out. If I was in a rush, forget it. I'd waste ten minutes trying to find a complete, functional container. I finally took the time to deal with it, matching tops to bottoms, and investing in quality click-top Tupperware to prevent leaks. Ever since, I've been a food-to-go pro, which saves ample time and money.

Go Green. Make good use of your sponges, rags, and dish towels. Instinctively reaching for napkins and paper towels to clean up every minor spill is not only a habit that harms the environment, but also one that becomes quite costly over time. Conserve water and energy by only running your dishwasher when it's full and unplugging small appliances like toasters and coffeemakers when they're not in use.

Use It! So many kitchens go unused in favor of meals out or quick and easy delivery. By learning to love your kitchen, your health (both physical and financial) will benefit.

Eating Out: Splurge Smarter

Eating in is an easy money saver, but it's not always an available option, nor is it always exciting. A nice restaurant meal can be a welcome and affordable indulgence if you follow these simple guidelines.

Set a Budget. Before you begin hunting for your dining locale, decide how much you're willing to spend. Setting a budget can help narrow your search significantly, particularly when you're in an unfamiliar place—traveling for business, on vacation, etc. A quick glance at the number of dollar signs on Yelp can be your first filter. Then double check menus online to make sure they're in line with your price point and appetite.

Coupon. Couponing isn't just for the grocery store. With services like Groupon and Restaurant.com, you can find discounts on everything from your corner bodega to the finest dining establishments in town. Sometimes, even the coupons themselves go on sale, meaning you can purchase a $25 restaurant voucher for just a few bucks!

Just like with any other coupon, be sure to read the fine print. Coupons generally have a number of restrictions, ranging from the dates and times they can be used to specific menu items they can be used for. You don't want to arrive at a restaurant anticipating filet mignon only to find that the coupon you have is applicable to a limited prix fixe menu of salad and chicken breast.

Opt for Lunch Specials. Midweek lunch specials are a great way to enjoy dining out without the evening and weekend pricing.

Save the Drinks for Later. Sticking to tap water during your meal can shave a significant amount off your total bill, and it's a better choice if you have to drive home afterwards. Once you're settled back home, enjoy a nightcap without the restaurant markup. Even non-alcoholic beverages like coffee and soda can increase your bill by quite a bit once the extra tax and tip are factored in.

Go to Happy Hour. If you're craving a pre-dinner cocktail, check out the happy hour specials. They're not always limited to alcohol, either. Oftentimes restaurants will have special food menus for happy hour or offer half-priced appetizers.

Try an Appetizer as an Entrée. Sometimes an appetizer may be enough for an entire meal. Look at the size of the dishes around you or ask your waiter how big the apps are to gauge whether you might be able to make a meal out of one of these smaller dishes.

Save Dessert for Later. Dessert is another treat to put off until you get home. Waiting will also give you a bit more time to digest your meal and see if you're still hungry for those extra calories.

Split It. It's no secret that restaurant portions are often two to three times the recommended serving size. By splitting your meal you can save on your health as well as your bill. If you don't have someone to share with, package the other half for later and make two meals out of one.

Consider Low Cost Cuisine. Certain types of cuisine are more affordable than others. For instance, noodle and vegetable-based cuisines like Chinese and Thai frequently offer excellent deals, whereas heavier, meat-based cuisines tend to carry a heftier price tag.

Double Check Your Bill. Not only should you make sure that your bill is accurate, but you should also note whether the specials and discounts that you used were applied correctly. Double check to see if the tip is included or if you need to leave your own. Remember to tip on the *pre-discounted* value of your meal. You're going for frugal, not cheap!

CHAPTER 8

———•———

Practical Savings:
Health & Wellness

One day, in the depths of winter, an offer for a free week-long trial membership to the local gym showed up in my mailbox. I was so relieved. I consider myself a year-round runner, but the unusually frigid weather and frighteningly slippery sidewalks had made it harder than ever to keep up with my standard workout routine. So as the polar vortex continued to blast outside, I took shelter at the gym down the street.

I had given up my gym membership four years earlier, so going back gave me a bit of culture shock. First of all, in a New York City gym, space is limited to say the least. The machines take up the entire floor, leaving only a tiny corner for stretching, BOSU balls, bands, light free weights, and mats. As I staked out a piece of floor to work with a medicine ball, I was surrounded by the gamut of gym culture; two girls Instagramming every moment of their workouts, a guy in a ripped t-shirt checking out everyone including himself, a girl in a crop top adjusting the fold of her yoga pants every two minutes—it was worse than a high school cafeteria.

Perhaps I've been spoiled by my outdoor runs. I'm so used to space, sunlight, wind, and even rain, as I listen to the sound of my breath and the occasional splashes off the East River. Rather than listening to blaring hip hop music and seeing everyone's deepest insecurities on display in the oversized gym mirror, I'm used to taking in the changing seasons as I run through familiar neighborhoods and scenes; soccer in the fall, quiet snowfall in the winter, blossoms in the spring, and endless varieties of activities and celebrations in the summer. Running has become an immersive experience in the cycles of life and culture. When I see other runners, there is a sense of community and shared understanding. Stepping into the gym could not have been more opposite. If I had to use a word to describe the overwhelming feeling that I had while I was there, it would be: *judgment.*

To make matters worse, I was approached twice during the first twenty minutes of my workout by trainers trying to recruit me for personal training sessions. I understand that's their job, but do they really expect me to pay an astronomical gym membership fee just to be harassed with sales pitches every morning while I work out? Suffice it to say, I am not a fan of the gym, for both practical and financial reasons.

Frugal Fitness: Run

Between the cardio blast, endorphin rush, vitamin D on your skin, and the total freedom of running outdoors, I can't think of a better way to exercise. (And I should know, I used to be a Certified Personal Trainer.) Besides the obvious health benefits, why do I love running so much?

Momentum. I've found that by challenging myself with new running goals—from running my first mile, to my first 5k, to my first half marathon, and finally, a full marathon—I've been able to create a sense of forward momentum in my life. Whether or not I meet my running goals is completely within my power, and that's empowering. While I might not have that same ability to control the other aspects of my life, I can take the momentum and empowerment that running gives me and let it permeate my life in a positive way.

It's Free. I haven't had to pay for a gym membership in years. I invest in a new pair of running shoes every year, but that's all I need. Races cost money, but they're a useful daily motivator and they pay off more than an unused gym membership ever will.

Make It Happen. If you're having trouble setting aside the time, use running as a mode of transit. For instance, if you're running an errand, literally *run it*—run to your destination and take the train home. Running is also a great way to explore a new city that you might be visiting. Just be sure to carry your ID, credit card, phone, and at least ten dollars for an emergency—or that impossibly cute coffee shop that you discover on your route that you simply have to try.

Frugal Fitness: YouTube Workouts

I love to have a workout video on hand when the weather keeps me from running or when I'm looking for a new way to tone or strengthen a certain part of my body. Luckily, there's no need to splurge on expensive fad programs like P90X or Insanity. YouTube has a vast array of fitness channels with various types of workouts available at your fingertips—all for free.

Here's a list of the top YouTube workout channels to help kick start your frugal fitness routine:

- Muscle and Strength Building: Scott Herman Fitness
  www.YouTube.com/ScottHermanFitness

- Pilates: Blogilates
  www.YouTube.com/Blogilates

- Yoga: Xen Strength Yoga
  www.YouTube.com/XenStrengthYoga

- General Workouts and Nutrition: Sarah Fit
  www.YouTube.com/SarahsFabChannel

- Fitness and Nutrition: Live Lean TV
  www.YouTube.com/BradGouthroFitness

Frugal Fitness: Free and Donation-Based Classes

Group fitness classes, from dance to yoga, allow you to be social while holding yourself accountable to your fitness goals. Unfortunately, group classes typically cost a minimum of twenty dollars a pop—not exactly budget friendly. Luckily, there are several ways to partake in these group sweat sessions on the cheap.

Free Trials and Introductory Specials. Before committing to an expensive package of classes, start with a free trial. Most workout studios offer a free class, or if you're lucky, a free week. Others will offer special rates to first time participants. The best way to stay on top of these promotions is to follow your local studios on social media for the latest deals and information.

Community Programing. Check your local newspaper, community center, and library to learn about fitness programs available in your area. Affordable fitness programming and events are generally a priority in most communities.

Athletic Stores. Popular fitness apparel stores like Lululemon and Nike sometimes host free fitness classes and events for the general public. Check the location nearest you or follow these companies on social media to get the most up-to-date schedule.

Search for Deals. Deal sites like Groupon, LivingSocial, and Amazon Local frequently offer discounts on fitness class packages. Some cities even have deal sites that focus exclusively on health and fitness services. To see what's available in your area, start with a simple Google search.

CHAPTER 9

Practical Savings: Personal Care

Do you know how much money you're spending on your appearance before you even get dressed in the morning? Everything from the moisturizer you apply after showering to your latest trip to the nail salon contributes to the massive amount of money that men and women spend each year on beauty products. It adds up quickly, but the good news is, it doesn't have to. You can maintain a polished look for a fraction of the cost. Cut your beauty bill by following these budget beauty tips.

D.I.Y. So much personal care and maintenance can be done at home on your own, both products and treatments alike. Waxing, threading, manicures, and pedicures are just a few of the regular services you can skip with little sacrifice or risk of failing. Thanks to the Internet, an endless array of natural ways to make everything from firming masks to hair conditioner is available to anyone with a WiFi connection. All you need are some basic kitchen staples and you've got yourself a chemical-free beauty solution for a fraction of the drugstore price.

Space Out Professional Visits. If your hairstyle is something that you simply can't sacrifice or style on your own, try rethinking your timeline. Even squeezing in an additional week between each coloring can mean one less salon visit each year—that's $100 in savings right there. If you only go for cuts, you can probably extend that timeline even more.

Get Creative. One of the best ways to save on your beauty routine is to make it less regimented. If you feel that you need to have a very specific product or service at a specific time at a specific place, you're not leaving yourself open to alternatives, which may be cheaper and sometimes even better.

When you receive a free product sample, use it and save yourself from having to buy a new mascara or lip gloss for a few months. When a new salon is offering an introductory special, give it a try instead of committing to your usual fixed-price stylist.

Be a Guinea Pig. High-end and low-cost meet in the world of hair modeling. You can get cuts, blowouts, and even color done for cheap, and sometimes free, when you allow your hair to be used for demonstrations, workshops, or classes at a beauty school. You needn't worry too much; sessions are almost always supervised by professionals.

This method isn't limited to hair, either. Massages, facials, and nails all have low or no-cost alternatives, as well. A simple web search for the treatment you'd like in the city you're in, along with the word "school," "free," or "cheap" can help you find a low-cost option near you.

Let Others Pay. If you have a tendency to draw a blank when people ask what you'd like for your birthday or an upcoming holiday, think about what you *need.* It could be something as basic as moisturizer or as indulgent as a massage. Gift cards are another great option because they give you the flexibility to spend where and when you need.

Decide What to Skip. You can make fun of Teri Hatcher's red wine baths or Angelina Jolie's caviar facials, as long as you're just as honest with yourself about your own unnecessary beauty rituals like eyelash extensions and tanning beds. It's great to feel pampered, but it's another thing to be wasteful.

Update Your Wardrobe for Less

Shop Your Closet. Mix and match what you already own. Chances are you've got a few pieces tucked away in the back of your closet that could use a little rediscovering.

Shop Seasonally. If you shop for a swimsuit just as the heat starts to set in, you'll pay for it, as prices generally hit their peak when demand is at its highest. End of season sales are the best times to score deals, meaning winter jackets in the spring and bikinis in the fall. If you can get yourself to think six months in advance, you'll benefit from a significant price drop.

Don't Pay Retail. Between coupons, sales, and clearance, there's no reason to pay full retail price. On your next shopping venture, use your smartphone to Google discounts and search price comparisons while you're in the store. If you can't find the deal that you want, snap a picture of the item's tag so you can search for a better deal later on.

Shop the Discount Chains. It seems that every discount chain from Target to Kohl's now carries several affordable designer lines. Pair those discounted prices with a coupon or sale to get the most bang for your buck.

Swap. Clothing swaps are a fun way to spend a frugal evening with friends while clearing out your closet and updating your wardrobe. To set up a swap, gather a group of friends and have them bring anything from their closets that they no longer want to keep. Include dresses, t-shirts, shoes, accessories...everything. Spend the evening trying on each other's discards. Whatever is left unclaimed at the end of the night gets donated. It's a win-win-win.

Check Out Sample Sales. If you're into designer labels, wait for the sample and trunk sales to stock up. When designers need to clear out the previous season's merchandise and sell clothing that didn't make the final production cut, they'll slash prices, making it at least somewhat affordable for the average consumer.

Go Online. eBay is a buyer's market. With so many sellers and an auction-based model, items are priced to sell. Just make sure that you're dealing with reputable sellers before placing a bid. If your item has a defect or doesn't fit quite right, you'll want to be able to return it to the seller for a full refund.

Beware of Outlet Malls. These can be a great place to snag deep discounts, but buyer beware. Some pieces are made specifically for the outlet mall, meaning they're not overstock, they're just lower quality.

Check the Kid's Section. Children's clothing is generally much cheaper than the adult equivalent. For basics like t-shirts and socks, see if you can find a better deal in the kid's section. Note: You'll have to figure out your child size first.

Thrift. If you have an uneasiness when it comes to "used" clothing, know that there are many different tiers of secondhand stores. While the Salvation Army and

Goodwill may require a bit more digging for quality wardrobe items, other consignment shops, like Second Time Around, have a strict pre-screening process. If the stigma of thrifting gets to you, remember, it's not "used," it's "vintage."

Choose Wisely. To save on future clothing costs, pick out timeless, versatile pieces. Consider which items will give you the most use for years to come. Blacks and beiges are always good colors to keep on hand; you can layer and accessorize to add pop and style for various occasions. Machine washables will also be cheaper than dry-clean-only items in the long run.

Thrifting

Of all my wardrobe savings strategies, thrifting is my absolute favorite. Despite dingy lighting and overwhelming piles of product, thrift stores are treasure troves for those who know *how* and *where* to look. Follow these tips to score exciting finds on your next thrift store trip.

Visit Often. Thrift stores don't carry standard merchandise, so what's available for sale largely depends on what's recently been brought into the store. Find out the days and times that your thrift store restocks its shelves to get first dibs on the latest items.

Check the Back Racks. Unlike a traditional retail environment, thrift stores don't typically carry multiples of an item. Some of the best pieces may be on the racks at the back of the store near the dressing rooms. These items have already been deemed valuable enough to try on. Just because they weren't a good fit for the person who originally found them doesn't mean they won't work for you.

Dress Appropriately. Not all thrift stores have dressing rooms, so be sure to wear tight fitting clothing in case you need to try on pieces over what you're already wearing.

Check Clothes Carefully. Check clothes for stains, loose threading, missing buttons, and other potential defects. Be sure to turn items inside out, too, for a full assessment. All damage should be noted before making a purchase. Can you fix it? Will it be worth the cost?

Ask for a Discount. This might be difficult at larger thrift stores, but remember, all retails shops need to get rid of items to clear the way for new inventory, so it's in their best interest to sell. If you notice a defect in an item, don't be afraid to point it out and ask for a lower price. Even if they can't change the price, maybe they'll throw in another small item for free.

Cash In on Deals and Specials. Many thrift stores offer discounts to certain groups, like seniors and students. They might also have special days or hours where items go on sale. To stay up to date on the latest thrift store deals and promotions, follow your favorite stores on social media.

Shop Seasonally. Similar to traditional retail, the best prices typically come at the end of the season. If you want to pick up cheap Christmas décor or patio furniture, go thrifting right after peak time when demand is low. The same holds true for clothing, which means you should shop for boots and jackets in April and beachy sundresses in September.

Consider the Neighborhood. Thrift store inventory comes from the surrounding neighborhood, so shop in areas where you admire the style. For instance, New Yorkers looking for "hip and trendy" should try Brooklyn, but for "chic and classic," the Upper East Side will be a better fit. Use the ThriftBuddy app to locate stores in your area.

Affordable Formal Wear

If, after rummaging through the depths of your closet, you find yourself with nothing to wear for the occasional upscale affair, implement these strategies to find fabulous *and affordable* formal wear.

Set a Budget. Before you begin your search for the perfect gown or suit, decide how much you can afford to spend. Don't fall prey to the *Say Yes to the Dress* syndrome, where every time you try on a beautiful dress you can't bring yourself to say "no," even when the price tag is twice your budget. Remember, your formal wear will likely be the least worn items in your closet, so don't allow the temptation of designer labels to cause you to overspend.

Keep It Classic. Unless you're buying a wedding dress, you'll likely wear your formal wear on more than one occasion. Sticking to classic styles and colors is best for repurposing. I've been able to wear the same dress to my senior prom and my best friend's wedding. While your 17-year-old princess self might be craving hot pink crinoline, a classic look is more practical in the long run. You can always add flare with shoes and accessories.

Think Seasonally. Formal attire goes on sale at the end of peak seasons. Get reduced prices on evening wear just after prom, wedding season, and the December holidays.

Shop Warehouse Sales. Warehouse sales are like sample sales, but on a much larger scale. Essentially, an entire store puts everything on clearance in an attempt to liquidate its excess merchandise. Be ready to sift through racks and boxes to find your perfect fit.

Shop Online. Find a formal outfit that you love and then comparison shop online at one of the many discount formal wear websites. Just make sure that you have accurate measurements and double check the return policy. Don't underestimate what a difference a few alterations and the right accessories can make.

Shop Secondhand Stores. Secondhand formal wear is generally barely used. There are only so many occasions that you need a gown or tux for, so it's not like purchasing secondhand shoes or jeans that were likely worn on a daily basis. By skipping the routine retail stops, you're also more likely to find a unique design that no one else is wearing.

Get a Rental. If you're into high-end labels and designer style, consider a service like Rent the Runway. Browse through dresses online by designers like Dolce & Gabbana, make a selection, and have it shipped to your door in two sizes to ensure the perfect fit. If you can't decide between two styles, you can rent a second dress of equal or lesser value for $25. With services like Rent the Runway, there's no reason that saving money and looking fabulous have to be mutually exclusive.

CHAPTER 10

—•—

Travel on a Shoestring Budget

Travel is one of those life experiences that people uniformly crave. Unfortunately, it has a tendency to be cost prohibitive, barring would-be explorers, adventure seekers, and life-learners from experiencing the world outside their small slice of home. But if you can train yourself to find travel and savings opportunities at every turn, you'll be amazed at how far you can travel on a limited budget.

Volunteer. There are many international volunteer opportunities that pay for the cost of travel. Some pay cash while others provide free room and board in exchange for services, but all are a fantastic way to become immersed in the culture and community of your destination while making a difference.

- *WWOOF (Worldwide Opportunities on Organic Farms)* pairs volunteers with farmers all over the world. Work a set number of hours on a farm in exchange for housing accommodations and three meals a day. Visit wwoofinternational.org.

- *Help Exchange* is a program similar to WWOOF. Work on a farm, ranch, lodge, hostel, or boat in exchange for food and accommodations. Visit helpx.net.
- *The Peace Corps* pays a small salary and offers benefits including health insurance. If you can make a two-year commitment and withstand a tough application process, the experience will undoubtedly be rewarding. Visit peacecorps.gov.

Work. Being a performer has given me access to many travel opportunities. What in *your* skill set might afford you the same prospects? Consider the following possibilities.

- Teach English as a Second Language (ESL): footprintsrecruiting.com
- Babysit or work as an au pair: aupair.com
- Become a flight attendant: theairlineacademy.com
- Work on a cruise ship: cruiseshipjob.com
- Join a yacht crew: findacrew.net, crewseekers.net
- Become a tour guide: backroads.com, dragoman.co.uk, trafalgartours.com, intrepidtravels.com
- For more career opportunities visit workanywhere.com

Reach Out to Friends, Family, and Acquaintances. In my experience, people are often happy to play host or hostess. A quick Facebook message to someone that I met fifteen years prior got me free housing and dinner when I visited Davis, California. An email to my childhood babysitter secured a place to stay in Seattle, plus a free tour and a long overdue reunion. Last time I was in Las Vegas, I saw two shows on the strip for free, courtesy of a former coworker from six years ago. The opportunities to reconnect with people that you haven't seen in years are endless, and they often become the best travel experiences of all.

Plan Around Obligations. If you find that your travel plans often revolve around work obligations, look for ways to capitalize on the opportunity—particularly if it's already being subsidized by your employer.

Tips for Practical Travel Savings

Use Travel Rewards. Always sign up for hotel, airline, and travel loyalty programs when you find them. Keep track of your accumulated discounts using a simple spreadsheet and update your balance at the end of each month.

Use Credit Card Rewards. (This strategy is only meant for responsible credit card users who pay their full balance each month.) Credit card rewards often come in the form of airline miles or hotel accommodations. If you've read the fine print and signed up for a rewards program, then use your credit card to leverage your normal spending and rack up tremendous discounts. *A word of caution, never use credit card rewards as a means to overspend for the sake of a freebie.*

Sublet Your Room While You're Away. Renting out a room is one of the easiest ways to make money with minimal effort. This simple strategy alone may pay for the entire cost of your trip. Visit Airbnb.com to assist in your search for a temporary renter.

Ask for Practical Gifts. When it comes to holidays and special gift giving occasions, practical gifting is not only a useful policy on the giving end, but also on the receiving end, too. By asking for practical items that you know you'll need, like cash and grocery store gift cards, you can free up money to spend on your "wants" later down the line—like your next vacation.

Read the Reviews. Not only will review sites help you determine and prioritize your must-do travel activities, but they also provide useful money saving tips. For instance, if you're visiting a state park, there may be free parking on the side of the road or in a nearby lot which will allow you to save money on vehicle entry fees. Or if you're going to see a musical or theatrical production, maybe there's a rush or standing room option that allows you to purchase tickets for a fraction of the price. A lot of these insider tips are shared on sites such as Yelp.com and TripAdvisor.com.

Check the Deals. Check the deal sites like Groupon and LivingSocial for the city you're traveling to. Not only will you discover what activities and dining options the area has to offer, but you'll find discounts, too.

Ask a Local. Avoid the tourist traps by asking locals for recommendations. You can either reach out to people that you know in the area or check online forums for insider recommendations. Get multiple opinions and see where you find the most overlap.

Do Lunch. Make lunch your big meal of the day. Most restaurants offer lunch specials, which means discounted prices on many of the same items that are served for dinner. The midday specials are an affordable way to experience the nicer and more popular restaurants in town without having to pay the dinner hour premium.

Happy Hour. Be sure to make a note of any happy hours or drink specials that you notice while researching the town or exploring it in person. When you're on vacation, there's no reason not to cash in on the drink specials that start at 4 p.m.!

Walk or Take Public Transit. Walking is one of the best ways to discover a new city. Pick up a free map at your hotel and be sure to ask about any areas that should be avoided. Most major cities also have excellent transit systems. If you can ride the bus or subway in your hometown, you can do it anywhere.

Have Fun. There's no point in vacationing if you're going to be worried about your budget the entire time. Plan ahead so that you know which activities are within your budget and where you can afford to splurge.

How to Prepare for Affordable Travel

Even after you've booked your travel accommodations and confirmed your reservations, there are a few more preparatory steps that should be taken to keep the overall cost of your trip within budget.

Call Your Bank. If you're traveling internationally, develop a plan for how you intend to withdraw local currency. Will you bring cash from home and then exchange it when you reach your destination? Will you withdraw local currency directly from an ATM? If using an ATM, do you have a debit card that will reimburse transaction fees worldwide? Do you have a credit card that allows you to make foreign transactions without a hefty fee? These are questions that you should answer at least four weeks before departure, so that you have ample time to make any necessary banking changes or preparations. Once you develop a plan, call each bank and credit card company that you do business with to inform them of your itinerary. Be sure to include dates and countries that you will be visiting. You don't want your credit card to suddenly stop working due to suspected fraudulent activity, leaving you financially stranded.

Decide on a Communication Strategy. Taking your cell phone abroad and "roaming" in a foreign country, even if it's only to access data, can add up to a substantial bill in a very short time. Consider downloading communication apps that run solely on WiFi like Skype, WhatsApp, and Google Hangouts, so that you can chat whenever you come across a WiFi hot spot. (To make sure that your cell phone doesn't accidentally pick up an expensive foreign data signal, put it in "airplane mode" from the moment you leave the U.S. to the time you arrive back home.)

Pack Smart. For domestic travel, most airlines now charge a fee for even a single checked bag. By traveling with only a carry-on, you can save at least $25 per flight. If you decide to check a bag, be sure to keep it below the designated weight limits; United and American Airlines charge $100 for each checked bag over fifty pounds. If you're traveling with a few heavy items, consider transferring them to your carry on to stay under the checked bag weight limit.

Consider Food. I take peanut butter just about everywhere I travel because I don't want to spend an extra five or ten dollars each day on breakfast. Trail mix? Granola bars? Nuts? Dried fruit? A few dollars saved on breakfast will free up money in your budget for a drink at happy hour, maybe even two!

Research. Knowing as much as possible about your destination, like how to navigate the city cheaply, is a major money saver. Besides, once you arrive at your destination, you don't want to waste time debating the relative value of each alternative—taxi, bus, train, etc. Do the research in advance so that you can maximize your play time while still making financially sound, value conscious decisions.

Couchsurfing and Rideshares

In the summer of 2012, I completed a conquest. I traveled for an entire week, spending as little money as possible. I began by venturing onto the site couchsurfing.org, where I created a profile and sent out requests. For those of you unfamiliar with *couchsurfing*, it's the practice of crashing on someone's couch for a night...or two...or however long you need—but instead of staying with a friend, you're staying with a total stranger. (The concept sounds crazy, I know.) So I thought I'd do some first-hand research and share my experience in an attempt to demystify and destigmatize the concept.

I wasn't entirely naïve. I understood that I was a small, 25-year-old female, traveling alone, asking to stay with strangers. So I narrowed my search to females and couples. My first stop was Provo, Utah. I typed the city name into couchsurfing.org's search engine and a multitude of potential hosts appeared on the screen before me. I sent requests to three members listing the dates that I'd be in town, and within thirty-six hours I had a place to stay.

Less than a week later I arrived in Provo, Utah. The couple that I was staying with had gone to see a movie, so I killed time at a local coffee shop until they returned home. Upon arrival, I introduced myself and we chatted for an hour or so before bed. They were Mormon newlyweds. We exchanged stories about life and our general travel experiences. Despite warnings that I might get a hard sell on the Latter-day Saints (Mormon) religion, the topic never came up—though there was a copy of The Book of Mormon strategically (or coincidentally) placed on my bedside table.

It was my first couchsurfing experience. I had no idea what to expect or what protocol to follow. I was amazed and grateful when my hosts showed me to my own room, complete with a twin bed and a set of clean towels. During my two-night stay in Provo, Utah, I slept well, washed up, ate, and tended to business—everything that I would have normally done at a hotel, but for free.

Next up, three days in Salt Lake City. I was confirmed to stay with a couple until they suddenly realized that I would be visiting on Mother's Day weekend. Because they had other commitments, they were forced to cancel. It was then that I encountered my first problem with couchsurfing: There are no guarantees. In a bind, I sent out more requests, this time broadening my search to include men. I heard back within a few hours.

My host picked me up and brought me to his home that he shared with his roommate. This time I was on the couch. I didn't mind, as it was a couch that I expected when I signed up to "couch" surf. After chatting for a bit, my host took me to downtown Salt Lake City where we spent the evening with his friends, visiting some local haunts. The next day they took me on a glorious hike through Utah's Wasatch Mountains. I bought groceries and made dinner for everyone as a way to thank them for their hospitality. On the third day, I had the place all to myself while my host went to work. Three nights on the couch did a number on my back, but it was free and worth every penny.

Next, I planned to travel to Omaha, Nebraska. Flights were far more expensive than I had anticipated, and getting a one-way car rental was almost as bad. So I hopped onto Craigslist to see what I could find. In the top left-hand corner of Craigslist is a section called "Community," where rideshares are listed. I browsed the ride offers and, sure enough, I found someone driving from Salt Lake City to Orlando, Florida—Omaha was right on the way.

I called and spoke to my rideshare to exchange driver's license numbers and confirm the details of our trip. We were to make the 14-hour drive in just a few short days. It would be the two of us along with a girl catching a ride to Miami. However, two days before our scheduled departure I received a text from my rideshare saying something was wrong with his vehicle, and we would have to postpone our trip by one day. But when the new departure date rolled around and I was waiting at the designated pickup location, I received another text saying the other girl hadn't shown up yet. After waiting for another thirty minutes, my ride finally arrived, but without the other passenger. Apparently, she was a no-show. So now it was just me and my rideshare, a gentlemen that I had just met, driving cross-country.

He seemed nice enough. We passed the first few hours getting to know each another. After nine hours I started getting stir crazy and counting down the miles to Omaha. Every so often it felt like the dilapidated car that we were driving was ready to give out—eventually it started making some disturbing noises. At 9 p.m., just as we were approaching Lincoln, Nebraska, an hour outside of Omaha, we had to make an emergency stop on the side of the road. The car was officially dying. My rideshare disappeared underneath the car for twenty minutes, trying to fix the unknown problem. Eventually we got back on the road, but I began to worry because my next couchsurfing hosts, who I had never met before, were expecting me by 11 p.m. Luckily we made it to Omaha just in time, and the 931-mile trip cost me only one tank of gas and a little bit of stress and worry.

When I arrived in Omaha, my host couple welcomed me with kindness and another room all to myself. They were in their mid-20s, a pair of high school sweethearts planning their upcoming nuptials. They had recently spent eight months traveling through South America, using couchsurfing.org to find places to stay. We traded stories—they talked about all the folks they'd hosted, including, most recently, a couple traveling through town for a Berkshire Hathaway conference. (Apparently couchsurfers range from drifters to investment bankers.) I spent the night on a full-size futon and let myself out in the morning. Another pleasant stay at no cost.

So in the end, would I recommend couchsurfing? Absolutely. Particularly for short stays. But be smart. Identify who you're comfortable staying with and read the profile of each potential host that you're considering. Additionally, there's a system of recommendations, similar to Yelp and TripAdvisor, where users can rate their experiences with hosts and surfers. I only contacted potential hosts who had received several positive reviews. But remember, there are no guarantees in couchsurfing.

As for rideshares, only consider this option if you have flexibility in your travel plans and can tolerate a certain level of uncertainty. The pros are that it's cheap and you get to meet new and interesting people. But the con is that, unlike couchsurfing, there's very little screening available—at least not on Craigslist. At the end of the day, saving money is great, but you have to do only what makes you feel safe and comfortable.

CHAPTER 11

—•—

Social Spending

As if it wasn't hard enough to battle your own vices and desires when trying to cut back on spending, there are many outside forces that make it all the more challenging—namely, cultural standards, societal expectations, and peer pressure from friends and family. Not to mention that you're young, fabulous, and ready to capitalize on life—#YOLO (you only live once), #FOMO (fear of missing out), and all of that other hashtag goodness.

While your relationships and life experiences are far more important than money, they're never an excuse to put your own financial health at risk. Friends may tempt you to overspend with promises of mind-blowing parties and unforgettable, life-changing getaways, but *you* are the one who will have to live with the financial consequences of your decisions. Sometimes, saying "no" to others, be it your closest family members or the societal standard as a whole, is the only way to say "yes" to yourself.

Societal Pressure: The Price of Being First

I've been trying to think of a time that I've willingly spent hours upon hours waiting in line to make a purchase. Admittedly, I've endured epic lines for job opportunities—in my case, auditions (think a lesser version of what they show on *American Idol* on a daily basis)—but those are lines that I tolerate for a chance to *make* money. I can't imagine being corralled like that to *spend* money, but it happens all the time. People camp out to purchase the latest game console, to get newly released brand name shoes, or, most notoriously, to get their hands on the latest innovation from Apple. While I don't think that I'll ever grasp the psychology behind that burning desire to be first (the thrill of it? improved social status?), I do find it fascinating what price people are willing to pay for that distinction.

Premium Prices. Waiting in line for the release of a new product or technology is the opposite of Black Friday. Instead of hoping to find a deep discount, customers are clamoring to pay top price.

It's amazing what a difference a little patience can make. Prices drop significantly over time, as products become more efficient and competitors release their own versions. When the iPad was originally released in 2010, it was priced at $499. I could walk into a store today, with no wait and no discount, and buy a better version of the iPad for $100 less.

The Cost of Evolution. Those who insist on being at the cutting edge of technology are paying top dollar for what they essentially consider to be a disposable product. Early adopters know how quickly technology evolves and how soon a revolutionary product can be replaced by a newer and better version, yet they still insist on paying a premium to be involved in the earliest stages of the product.

I didn't buy an iPod until the iPod touch came out, and I haven't had to buy a new iPod since. I waited until the technology evolved to a place where its form and function would serve me for years to come; not just entertain me with its novelty for a few months. The first generations of products and technologies are always imperfect. It takes time and often several new versions to work the kinks out.

Time Cost. In September of 2013, with the launch of Apple's *seventh* iPhone (the 5c and 5s), there were lines at Apple stores around the world from China to New York. Those who weren't willing to give up their own time hired stand-ins to wait in line for them; $55 for four hours was the going rate on TaskRabbit.com. Of course, those who had the patience to wait until the next day got the *same* product for the *same* price without the cost of waiting in line. Those who had enough patience to wait even longer undoubtedly saw lower prices and even less waiting time.

The Price of Being Last

Between the costs of waiting in line and paying top dollar for imperfect technology, there are plenty of reasons to hold off on buying the latest gadgets. But it's also important to consider the point at which *waiting* to upgrade technology or purchase a new device can actually *cost* you money.

Until a year ago, I had a flip phone. You remember those, right? They were the objects where you'd have to hit the number "2" button three times just to type the letter "F." Yeah, one of those. I went about my day happily unconnected to the Internet, saving myself a great deal of money each month by not requiring an expensive data plan.

But a few months before I made the switch to a smartphone, I started to experience what some now refer to as #FOMO or "fear of missing out." Unfortunately, my #FOMO was not just superficial anxiety—it was real, I *was* missing out. When I'd arrive home at the end of a long day, my inbox would be flooded with audition requests and follow up opportunities that I had missed out on because I hadn't checked my email in time. Without constant access to what had become *standard* data service, I literally couldn't do my job effectively.

As much as we'd all like to feel unplugged every so often, being connected to the latest information, data, and technology makes us more valuable—more able to provide a quick response, draw upon resources, and be informed in a pinch. Just imagine how far behind you'd be if you had never adopted that late 20th century fad known as the Internet!

You May Be Falling Behind the Times If...

Everyone Else Is Doing It. Although it's not always in your best interest to follow the crowd, in terms of business and communication advances, if you don't follow close behind, you will undoubtedly be left in the dust. You don't need to have the latest and greatest technology or product, but you need to have access to the same functions that everyone else is using.

People Are Asking. Undoubtedly, the tool that you need the most is the one that you're always being asked for. If customers are constantly inquiring about your website, perhaps it's time to build one.

You're Missing Out. As with my experience, if you find yourself repeatedly missing out on opportunities, then you need to find a better way to stay relevant and in touch.

You're Confused. If common words in the modern vernacular like "blog" or "IP address" make your head spin, it's time to do research and get back up to date.

Cultural Pressures

Just as societal pressures can influence spending in sometimes necessary, but often frivolous ways, so can cultural and community expectations. I come from a very tightly-knit Ukrainian community—not in the sense that I was born abroad, but in the sense that I grew up speaking the language, attending countless community events, being a part of several cultural organizations, and developing lifelong friendships with fellow Ukrainians. (Use the movie *My Big Fat Greek Wedding* as a reference point.) There are definitely financial implications when you're part of that kind of community—both good and bad.

The Pros...

Support. When you have hundreds of genuine friendships, there's a huge network of support. When raising money for my NYC Marathon run for cancer research, most of the donations came from within my community network. When I've needed help through a tough time, there were many people ready to offer anything that I could possibly need—a place to stay, a hot meal, or a stiff drink (we Eastern Europeans love our vodka).

Network. The benefits of my cultural network extend far beyond my immediate NYC community. I've enjoyed free stays and meals at the homes of friends in Chicago, Lake Tahoe, and even Ukraine. My network also comes in handy in managing my day-to-day life. With such a widespread community, an entire range of professions and skills are represented. I've benefited from free doctor visits, complimentary dental cleanings, and even job opportunities, all due to cultural connections.

The Cons...

Traditions and Expectations. As part of a community that prides itself on tradition, there are many expectations, some of which carry a hefty price tag—joining organizations, attending expensive events, and contributing to cultural institutions, to name a few.

Peer Pressure. Those who don't share the experience of a restricted income don't understand the reality of limited funds. The peer pressure to spend, combined with traditions and expectations, can be a major budget strain.

Impossibly Large Social Circles. As much as I love a good party, there is *always* an event to attend, and it doesn't always come cheap—fundraisers, holiday weekends, debutante balls (yes, we have debutante balls), etc. Also, those hundreds of close friends that I mentioned before are all approaching the age of marriage. With the average cost of attending a wedding topping $500, I could be practically bankrupt in a few years...

How to Handle Financial Peer Pressure

Share Your Financial Goals and Priorities. If you're like me, then you may find that you can't afford to attend every party, event, or happy hour that you're invited to. Rather than feeling pressured to spend money that you don't have, prioritize what you *can* afford to do and explain your decision honestly to your peers. By being direct, your friends and family will likely support you rather than pressure you into spending money that doesn't align with your financial goals and priorities.

Offer an Alternative. If you can offer a low-cost alternative to an expensive activity, then you'll be able to spend more time with friends and family without jeopardizing your budget. Even if a meal or activity is already planned, take it upon yourself to research promo codes, coupons, and group rates. With a little extra effort, you may be able to find savings for everyone involved, including yourself.

Just Say "No." Sometimes the best option is to opt out of a group activity or meal that is beyond your price range. Don't be afraid to explore on your own while your peers venture elsewhere. By picking and choosing which group activities to partake in, you can still be involved, but on your own terms.

Avoid These Financial Faux Pas

Although you want to keep social spending in line with your budget priorities, don't let money dictate your social calendar or jeopardize your relationships. If you truly value your loved ones, steer clear of these financial faux pas.

Always Being the Flake. Are you the one who always leaves your wallet at home or doesn't have enough cash to cover your tab? Mistakes happen, cash runs out, and things are forgotten, but if your friends consistently wind up having to cover your financial blunders, they *will* start to resent you.

Always Having to Be Asked. If a friend loans you money, for whatever reason, in whatever amount, pay it back as soon as possible. Don't put your friend in the uncomfortable position of having to *ask* to be repaid. Take the initiative and get to an ATM or begin making payments immediately.

Spending Frivolously While You're in Debt. What your friend *won't* appreciate is waiting on that loan repayment while you go shopping for a fancy new tablet or take a luxury vacation. Debts to friends are still real debts, even if they come without interest.

Never Repaying. If you've been delinquent repaying a loan from a friend, shame on you. It's one thing to be upfront about unforeseen circumstances that halt or slow down the repayment process, but it's another to stop communicating and making an effort altogether. The way that you treat a loan from a friend reflects the value that you place on your friendship.

Social Spending "Obligations"

Almost everything that we spend money on is by choice. Yes, we have needs, but we *choose* those needs. Yes, there are expectations, but we *choose* which expectations we care to meet.

When it comes to social, cultural, and familial obligations, there's a lot of *"I have to"* justifications toward spending. These obligations are typically a duty or commitment to which you *feel* bound, not something to which you *are* bound—an important distinction.

For example, let's say that my best friend asked me to be a bridesmaid. I would feel a strong sense of commitment, but I would not accept until I understood the full financial implications. Would I be expected to purchase a dress? Accessories? Attend other bridal events? What would be the total cost? If I were to assume that I'd be paying the average cost of being a bridesmaid, which according to WeddingChannel.com is $1,695, I would have to decline, regardless of my sense of obligation. And yet, many people would make the opposite decision by allowing their sense of obligation to overtake their financial reality.

My challenge to everyone, and to myself, is to never use the phrase *"I have to"* when it comes to spending money. Although you may feel a strong sense of commitment to yourself and others in various circumstances, at the end of the day, the things that you spend money on are *your choice*. If we can each accept that truth, perhaps we'll more wisely weigh our financial reality against our own sense of obligation in the future.

Obligatory Spending: Weddings

"Weddings are not fundraisers, invitations are not invoices." – Jodi R.R. Smith, founder of the etiquette consulting firm, Mannersmith.

I love weddings—eating, drinking, and dancing in the company of my best friends and family. Nothing could be better.

So what's not to love? … *The cost.*

Wedding culture has evolved to include unprecedented spending expectations. Showers and engagement parties have turned into mini-weddings, bachelorette parties have become multi-day destination events, and weddings themselves now cost nearly thirty thousand dollars on average. I'm all for celebrating, but the mere cost of participating in a wedding has completely surpassed what I can afford!

If You're the One Planning the Wedding...

Keep It in Perspective. If you're going to have multiple events—engagement party, wedding shower, bachelor/bachelorette party, wedding, and post-wedding brunch—think in terms of the total cost to attend each event and see where you may be able to keep it casual. Perhaps a backyard BBQ for the shower or a weekend camping trip for the bachelor party?

Don't Be Offended. If you want to have a lavish destination wedding or an over-the-top celebration, go for it, it's your day. But don't be offended if people decline. I may love you, but not more than I love having a roof over my head!

If You're Invited...

Assess and Prioritize. Before RSVP'ing to a wedding event, be sure to add up all of the associated costs to see if it's within your budget. This might mean calling the hotel for room prices, calculating travel costs, and reaching out to the maid of honor to ask for a breakdown of bachelorette party costs. Once you run the numbers, you may need to opt out of certain events or search for cheaper alternatives like staying at a different hotel, not staying overnight, etc.

Don't Be Afraid to Say "No." I want to celebrate every moment of "wedding mania" with my girlfriends—partly because it's a blast and partly because I love them and want to support them. But when the financial strain is too much, it's time to say "no." Remember, obligations are choices, too.

Don't Overspend. Once you've committed to participating in a wedding, make sure that you stay within your budget. If you're headed out on the town for the bachelorette party, withdraw your spending limit *in cash* so that you're not tempted to spend more, especially once the booze starts flowing.

Don't Overgift. The price of your wedding gift should not be determined by the price of your plate, as is the common, misguided advice. Just because your friend has expensive taste doesn't mean that you should feel pressured to match his or her spending choices. Remember, a wedding invitation is not an invoice. The price of your gift should be determined by your budget and your relationship with the couple. (Purchasing a group gift is a convenient way to give a nicer item from the registry without taking on the high price tag alone.)

Be Creative. Consider gifts like monogrammed towels or custom stationery as creative (and inexpensive) personalized gifting alternatives. Or, if you know the couple well, consider gifting them an experience like a class or a food tour that you know they'll enjoy. Finally, consider using your skills to save on spending by offering a service that the happy couple needs. Perhaps you can help with dress alterations, bake the cake, or edit the wedding video? It's better for your gift to be thoughtful and less expensive than to damper the celebration with a heavy load of financial anxiety!

Obligatory Spending: Holidays

I consider myself a pretty awesome gift giver. I think that it's because I hate the idea of spending money on something that won't be used or enjoyed. While my budget seriously restricts how often I can give a gift (or give the gift that I want), I love to share in the joy of gifting. Here are my practical tips for how to give the perfect gift.

Give Something Practical. I hate "tchotchkes." Unless your giftee is a collector, there's no use in giving figurines, coins, stuffed animals, and other pointless clutter. If you don't want your gift to wind up in storage or the trash, give a practical gift.

Does your giftee have any hobbies? Has she had any recent life changes (moved to a new city, switched jobs, etc.)? What could you buy to support her interests and fulfill her latest needs? Maybe the makings of a new wardrobe to celebrate a recent weight loss, or the latest fancy kitchen tools for a cooking aficionado, or a collection of earrings for your girlfriend who always seems to lose one.

Even the most mundane things can make wonderful gifts—a haircut, a cleaning service, groceries, laundry pick up and drop off—all of the things that you have to take care of yourself, but are so much nicer when they're taken care of for you. As long as you gift something that can be used, you can't go wrong.

Give an Experience. Tangible gifts can rarely compare to an experience that you give or share with someone that you love. On a limited budget you can give the gift of time and make a special evening at home. Or, if you can afford to, consider taking a class (cooking, pottery, yoga, etc.), getting a couples massage, seeing a show (theatre, improv, concert, comedy), or even giving a vacation—the ultimate gift in my opinion!

Give Something Thoughtful (or Priceless). Ideally, every gift should be thoughtful, but when you're truly cash strapped or you want to create a more personal experience, thoughtfulness is the way to go—photo collages, illustrated frames, scrapbooks, edited homemade movies, self-authored stories, and so on. Think of how much meaning your wedding video has (or will have) for you, or the sentimental value that family heirlooms have. That's the power of a personalized, thoughtful gift. It's priceless.

If you're not particularly crafty yourself, check out sites like Etsy.com and Fiverr.com. I've used these sites to buy everything from professional logos to personalized organic soaps, all for just five bucks!

Think "Little Indulgences." If you know your gift recipient well enough, you may be able to brainstorm a few reasonably priced *wants*. Think about the little indulgences your giftee likes to splurge on from time to time but knows she shouldn't. Maybe a manicure? Name brand coffee? Movie tickets? A certain grab-and-go food spot?

Give a Taste. In general, you should avoid giving a gift that requires your giftee to spend her own hard earned money to maintain or supplement it. But there are options for giving a "little taste" of what's available and leaving it up to your giftee to spend more.

For instance, when I moved to a new apartment, my friend gave me $10 gift certificates to a few restaurants in my neighborhood, so that I would get a taste of my new surroundings. You can also "give a taste" in a less literal sense by giving a one month subscription to a service like Netflix or Spotify.

Start a Giving Account

By saving steadily over a period of time, the costs of holidays and events are easier to endure. I recommend starting a "giving account" and contributing between 1 to

5 percent of each paycheck into the account throughout the year. You can draw from the account for giving occasions like holidays, birthdays, and weddings, and to make charitable donations, too.

While you shouldn't spend a penny more than what you have saved in your giving account, feel free to spend *less*. Use the extra money to contribute to your 401(k) or make an extra mortgage payment. Also, don't forget events that will be coming at the beginning of the following year. If you wipe out your entire account in December, there won't be anything left to give in January.

Obligatory Spending: Generosity and Quid Pro Quo

I like to think that relationships are about love and support rather than keeping tabs and quid pro quo. But when financial resources come into play, the reality of tit for tat and the question of fairness inevitably comes to the surface, particularly when it comes to giving.

I often think of singletons who never marry or have children. They're constantly giving—for weddings, baby showers, friends' children's birthdays—but never do they benefit from equal reciprocity. It might be crass to suggest "keeping score" when it comes to generosity, but it's hard to ignore the inequity of it all. On the other hand, arguing "equality" when it comes to gifting seems to defeat the purpose. Perhaps it's the culture of gifting that needs more scrutiny—the expectations and feelings of obligation.

How about those moments where you've given a thoughtful homemade scrapbook, but you receive a fancy new iPod in return? I don't know about you, but it all makes me very uncomfortable. Whether it's spoken or not, I often feel that underlying sense of quid pro quo when it comes to gift giving. There are, however, a few tactics I've used to help mitigate these uncomfortable moments.

Draw Names. When it comes to gift giving within a family or circle of friends, drawing names can help relieve the pressure of figuring out how you're going to budget for multiple gifts. Rather than the singleton having to buy for each member of a large family and getting one group gift in return, each person in the hat participates in equal measure.

Set Limits. Setting clear spending limits as well as placing limits on when gifts will (or won't) be given, can be very helpful. For instance, gifts will only be given for the first baby shower, holiday gifts will be capped at $50, etc.

Be Honest. To avoid resentment or misunderstanding, I always strive to remain as open as possible with my financial realities and priorities. The fact is, if someone gives me a fancy gift valued at several hundred dollars, they know that I won't be able to reciprocate the gesture, no matter how much I care about and love them.

Social Spending Pressure: Keeping Up with the Joneses

You know the Joneses, right? They're the ones you're always struggling to keep up with. They have the bigger house, the better car, the nicer…everything. In the world of personal finance and frugal living, "keeping up with the Joneses" is a dangerous game. It leads to lifestyle inflation and living beyond your means, often to the detriment of your financial present and future.

The alternative to "keeping up with the Joneses" is to "live simply," a lesson that I've taken to heart. Finding the richness and joy in the little things is something that I pride myself on—frugal is fabulous and broke can be beautiful.

The benefit of "living simply" is that it keeps my expenses low; affording me the opportunity to fund the continued pursuit of my dreams while still preparing for a bountiful financial future. Occasionally I'll be tempted to lead a fancier life by a drool-worthy fine dining menu or an enticing retail display at Pottery Barn, but I'm generally good about recognizing that desire to "keep up with the Joneses" as an unnecessary and unconstructive urge.

But even I, in my infinite condemning of overspending and hyperconsumerism, fall prey to the dangers of lifestyle inflation. I admit that I have dreams of owning a sprawling beachside property complete with gourmet kitchen, walk-in closets, jet skis, and the like. With reality shows like *Million Dollar Listing* and a Facebook news-feed full of photos from friends in exotic international locales, it's no wonder. The Joneses are no longer the family next door in suburban USA with the white picket fence; they're now the ones with fabulous penthouse apartments who are taking trips around the world.

Inflated Lifestyle Reference Points

Advertising and media exacerbate the problem of who we now consider the Joneses to be. For example, *Friends* and *Sex and the City* were two major influences that shaped my assumption of the New York City standard of living. (You mean that I *can't* afford a huge apartment in the West Village as a waitress or one column writer?)

Non-fictional media figures also play an influential role. What I wouldn't give to have the lifestyle and wardrobe of Michelle Obama or Kate Middleton. But by using millionaire reality stars or unrealistic fictional lifestyles as my reference point for the things that I want and need, I set myself up for lifestyle inflation that far exceeds my limited means.

The Joneses, with means so far beyond our own, have become the social norm, redefining and ratcheting up the "minimum" standard of living. The list of wants transforming into needs is expanding at an unprecedented rate, and we simply can't afford to keep up with it. The white picket fence is no longer enough when the McMansion is the new normal.

In 1986, the Roper Center for Public Opinion Research asked Americans what income they needed to earn in order to fulfill all of their dreams. The answer was $50,000. By 1994, that level had more than doubled, from $50,000 to $102,000. Just imagine what that number would be today, twenty years later!

How to Stop Lifestyle Inflation

To stop lifestyle inflation, you first need to decide *who are your Joneses?* Will you live a life of constant dissatisfaction, feeling like you never have enough because you can't possibly spend on par with millionaire reality stars? Or will you model your lifestyle after those who prioritize their time and experiences over possessions and things? Or maybe you'll fall somewhere in the middle. Upon further reflection, I admit that I still want the beachfront experience, but maybe I can give up the fantasy of a palatial estate that would mire me in debt. Instead, I'll get my fulfillment from my friends and family who will share the scenery and ocean breeze with me.

CHAPTER 12

———•—•———

Break Free of Broke

I've never believed in judging the financial stature of others based on their income alone. Surely living below your means and establishing patterns of saving and investing for the future are more far important than whatever your present income might be. However, there comes a point where you max out that side of the equation—there are only so many ways that you can save. However, the potential for increased earnings, the other side of the equation, is practically limitless.

I must confess that I've remained stagnant on the income side of my equation for quite some time. While those around me continue to see their paychecks rise, I seem to be locked into where I've been for the past few years. I'm able to cover my expenses, travel, maintain an emergency fund, and contribute to my Roth IRA, but not much else.

You may be thinking, "You can pay your bills and save for the future, what else could you possibly need?" Well, how about something *more.* I have bigger dreams, too; namely, a home, a family, and the basic pursuit of "evolutionary happiness." I wouldn't call it lifestyle inflation as much as I'd call it maturation.

With the additional expenses and priorities of having a mortgage, a car, and a child, all needing to be funded from my income, I would no longer be able to contribute to my IRA or savings. In fact, I'd be at risk of needing to rely on debt just to keep my head above water. The reality is that if my income doesn't mature as I do, then I go from being a fiscally responsible young adult to a debt-spiraling middle-aged woman in no time.

While I may not be broke right now, I often *feel* broke because my options are limited by my income. I can continue to reduce my expenses and find new ways to save, but even saving 100 percent of my limited income won't be enough to fund the pursuit of my American Dream. Until I find a way to increase my income to the point that I no longer feel limited in my life choices, I will forever feel broke.

The Make or Break Number

The entirety of my financial philosophy can be reduced to what I call the "make or break number." It's the number that allows you to break the cycle of living from paycheck to paycheck and affords you the opportunity to follow your dreams. Knowing your make or break number is the first step to breaking free of broke forever.

So, do you know what *your* make or break number is? That is, do you know exactly how much it costs, at a bare minimum, to run "YOU, Inc."? You must know your number, as it serves as a benchmark for the financial viability of your life. It serves as a guide for what opportunities you can afford to take and which you can't afford to pass up.

To calculate your make or break number, put together a bare-bones survival budget. This is the budget that only includes necessities and eliminates all discretionary spending. Think of anything that you can safely, smartly, and sustainably live without for a month, without disrupting your ability to live and work. Your survival budget should include items like food, housing, transportation, insurance, taxes, and even basic Internet and cell phone if these serve as critical work tools.

Next, on top of your survival budget, you must add four additional elements.

1. A 10 percent buffer to include expenses that you failed to account for
2. Emergency fund savings amount
3. Retirement savings amount
4. Debt repayment amount (if you're in debt)

Once you add the full cost of these essential add-ons to your survival budget, you'll have your make or break number. Know what your number is on an annual, monthly, weekly, and even daily basis.

When you start prioritizing one of the elements that comprise your make or break number over any of the others, you've reached the breaking point. For example, when you find yourself having to choose between food and housing, or retirement contributions and insurance premiums, you're in trouble.

To ensure that you never reach your breaking point, your income needs to remain above your make or break number at all times. It serves as a guide for the bare minimum that you can afford to earn without having to dip into your emergency fund. Any earnings above and beyond your make or break number can be allocated at your discretion.

If your income falls short of your make or break number, you have two options.

- *Option 1. Find a way to reduce your essential expenses.* Is it possible to cut back on any of your must-have survival expenses? Can you find a roommate, begin couponing, or switch to a less expensive phone plan?
- *Option 2. Earn more money.* Either ask for a raise, find a new job, or take on additional income ventures.

How to Earn More Money

The first step to earning more money is to ask yourself, "What do I have to offer? What can I do, make, or provide that has monetary value?" As you consider your answers, keep in mind that even if your income exceeds your make or break number today, it never hurts to have extra income. Here are my favorite conventional (and unconventional) ways to create additional income:

Sublet a Room

For those of you living in an apartment the size of a closet, this may not be a practical option. But for those of you who have a spare bedroom and are looking to generate extra income, consider subletting a room. If you're not comfortable with the idea of having an extra person in your living quarters for the foreseeable future, list your room on Airbnb.com or Roomorama.com and set short-term availability.

While subletting can be financially beneficial, there are reasons to be cautious. You're leaving your home and, presumably, your belongings in the hands of another person, so proceed carefully and follow these basic subletting guidelines.

Check the Sublet Laws in Your State. Rules regarding sublets and your right to do so as a leaseholder vary from state to state. Check your local sublet laws to make sure that you're in compliance.

Be Upfront with Your Landlord. If I disappeared for a few months and a stranger was going in and out of my apartment, I would hope that my landlord would take notice. It's best to be upfront and let your landlord know that you plan to sublet, so that your apartment and building can remain secure.

Find a Trustworthy Subletter. I've been lucky to find subletters that are almost always within one or two degrees of separation from myself. Facebook has been my greatest tool in this regard. Post a status update. If your friends don't need a place to stay, they might know someone who does.

Connect with Your Subletter. Ideally, you should meet with your subletter to get to know each another and familiarize yourselves with the space and your expectations of how the space should be treated. If you can't meet in person, you should (at a minimum) chat over the phone to establish a connection and talk through sublet details. You want to make sure that your apartment and everything in it will be secure with whomever you're subletting to. Establishing trust, rapport, and mutual expectations is paramount.

Execute a Sublease with Your Tenant. In addition to a verbal agreement, it's important to put the terms of your sublease in writing. A written agreement protects both you and your subletter by detailing each party's rights and responsibilities. Here's a partial list of items to include in a sublease agreement:

- Full names of both parties and their respective roles in the agreement.
- Identify the property, how it is to be used, and any restrictions. (For residential purposes only, no roof or garage access, etc.)
- Identify the term of the sublease by including both start and end dates.
- State the amount of rent to be paid. Include specifics such as how much, how often, in what form, and to whom payments will be made. Be sure to include a penalty for late payments, too.
- State the amount of the required security deposit. List the conditions that must be met for the deposit to be returned and include reasons why it may be withheld. (Damage to the furniture, late payment of rent, nonpayment of utilities, etc.)
- Sign and date the contract. Make sure that you each have a copy of the executed contract.

If the process of subletting a room seems overwhelming, consider renting out something smaller like a spare closet or parking space. Remember, generating extra income is all about what you have to offer. Take inventory and figure out how you can turn your offerings into income generators.

Sell Your Stuff

How many articles of clothing do you have that you've barely worn? Did you just move in with your significant other and now find that you have doubles of practically everything from dishes to end tables? Do you have stacks of books that you've already read just laying around your house collecting dust? If you own something of value that you no longer use, consider selling it on eBay, Craigslist, Amazon, or even Facebook.

Admittedly, selling home furnishings and other personal items is easier said than done. I tried my hand at selling items on eBay and I learned some valuable lessons in the process. Namely, I learned…

Listing Items Is Time Consuming. Not only do you need to take a picture of the item you're attempting to sell, upload it, and write a full description, but you need to do this for *each item* in your collection. You also need to do thorough research to determine the correct asking price. What's the item selling for around the web and what price can you expect based on its present condition?

It's Hard to Sell. I've only been able to sell around 20 percent of the items I've listed online—most of which only sold after relisting them several times at lower prices.

Packing Is a Pain. You'll need to have some packing supplies on hand, but don't preemptively buy a car full of packing peanuts when you don't even know that your items are going to sell. Of course, when you *don't* buy packing supplies in bulk, they tend to be quite pricey, so there's really no winning.

Shipping Is Expensive. I do not recommend giving customers a free shipping option unless you're familiar with current shipping rates. Due to some unfortunate estimates on shipping expenses, I've cost myself quite a bit of money.

Don't Forget the Costs of Selling. If you don't expect to sell your item for at least $25, it might not be worth your time and effort to list it. I've spent several hours taking pictures of items, listing them, packaging them, and taking them to the post office to ship, all for a $5 profit after eBay fees and PayPal fees are deducted.

For smaller, less valuable items, try selling them via social media outlets like Facebook. With fewer fees and far less competition, you may have a bit more luck turning a profit. Don't forget good old-fashioned options like garage sales and sidewalk sales, too. For anything that you can't sell, donate it and enjoy a small tax deduction.

Provide a Service

If you find yourself with nothing to do on an evening or weekend, keep your eye out for service opportunities like babysitting, housekeeping, or dog walking. Babysitters in some metropolitan areas can command prices as high as $25 per hour. In other words, four hours of reading *The Hunger Games* while little Johnny sleeps can earn you a hundred bucks. Check out Sittercity.com for jobs in your area—they also list tutoring and housekeeping jobs, too. If you have specialized skills like programming, editing, carpentry, or plumbing, you can probably command an even higher rate.

If you don't have a special skill to turn into income, consider registering for focus groups in your free time. If you fit the criteria, you can make up to $100 for an hour or two of your time—just for offering your opinion. To find focus groups, visit FindFocusGroups.com.

Become a Micro-Entrepreneur

Thanks to the power of the Internet, you can now offer your goods and services to a broad range of people all over the world. Start your own business or earn a few extra dollars with some of these options.

Use Your Car as a Rental or Taxi Service. Use a service like Lyft, RelayRides, Uber, or Getaround to earn extra money just by renting out your vehicle or serving as a taxi driver for the afternoon.

Become a Tour Guide. Tourists are willing to pay a premium for an insider's guide to a new city. Be that insider and earn extra cash while meeting new and interesting people. Become a tour guide in your town by using the service Vayable.

List Your Product or Service and Your Price. Are you a graphic artist who enjoys designing corporate logos in your spare time? Do you know how to write code or build websites? Are you willing to wait in line on behalf of a stranger for hours (or days) to buy the latest iPhone? List your product and service, along with your fee, using a service like Elance, Fiverr, Gigbucks, oDesk, TaskArmy, or TaskRabbit.

Make Your Hobbies Work for You. If you love photography, sell your images on stock photo sites like iStockphoto.com and GettyImages.com. If you love shopping, sign up to be a mystery shopper. If you love crafts, sell your work or take custom orders on Etsy. You get the idea... The best part is, by making your hobbies work for you, you're guaranteed to love what you're doing.

Rent Out Just about Anything. From bikes to tools, online rental marketplaces like Loanables and Zilok make renting out just about anything an income producing reality.

Sell Your Hair. This is definitely not the most conventional way to earn extra income, but it's too easy and profitable not to list. Your hair can fetch anywhere from $300 to $900 on a site like Hairwork.com. (On that note, you can also sell your sperm or eggs for a pretty penny, but there's a lot more to consider when selling your "reproductables.")

When to Side Hustle

Side hustles cover the full spectrum of income producing possibilities—from babysitting to freelance writing to web design to soap making—basically anything that you can charge money for can become a side hustle.

As a professional actress, I've had to become a side hustling pro to sustain myself through periods of un- and underemployment. Through my personal experience, I've learned that side hustles are prone to good times and bad. By identifying the best times to side hustle, you'll be able to maximize your extra earnings and avoid a great deal of frustration and wasted effort.

The Best Times to Side Hustle…

At the Last Minute. Nothing gives you the upper hand in a negotiation quite like your services being desperately needed as soon as possible. Leaving yourself open to side hustle opportunities that pop up at a moment's notice may not always be convenient, but it can pay off big. Not only are you in a position to negotiate a better rate, but you can specify any additional terms that you may find beneficial—certain hours, breaks, rush fees, etc.

Holidays and Special Occasions. I was once asked to babysit for a New Year's Eve party. I didn't get to kiss someone special at the stroke of midnight, but about an hour later I walked away with $300 in my pocket. If you're willing to give up some of your regular traditions or even a few weekend nights, you can charge a premium for your time.

The Worst Times to Side Hustle...

When Preparation Takes Too Long. If your side hustle involves some kind of preparation or travel in order for you to provide your service, it may not be worth your time if you're not guaranteed a minimum amount of work. For instance, if you were asked to babysit for two hours, but you had to commute an hour each way, would it be worth four hours of your time for only two hours of pay?

When You're Unemployed. Oddly enough, side hustling when you're unemployed doesn't always make financial sense. If you take on part time work while collecting unemployment, you have to report your income and give up a quarter of your weekly unemployment pay for each day that you work, no matter how few hours or how small the earnings. For example, if you collect $400 per week in unemployment, and you're offered a babysitting job for one day, you would have to earn at least $100 babysitting—otherwise you'd be operating at a loss. Yes, it seems counterintuitive to discourage people from working, but unfortunately that's how the system works.

When You're Exhausted. Working a full-time job in addition to cultivating a side hustle, along with everything else that you do, like working out, pursuing hobbies, and raising a family, is *a lot* to handle. Sometimes, taking a break is more valuable than constantly filling your time with more work—even if it means less money in the short term.

How I Earn My Living

In order to keep my schedule open for auditions and performance opportunities, I avoid jobs in the traditional nine-to-five realm and focus on side hustles instead. To make ends meet I've done everything from host a trade show at Comic Con to administer a department at a musical theatre conservatory. My goal isn't to indulge you in stories from my various jobs, but to share how I've built and maintained an arsenal of income-producing side hustle options. Here are my top recommendations to anyone trying to do the same.

Be a Nice Person. I could have called this point "networking," but there's something inherently impersonal and limiting about that word. I've found that when you treat others well, opportunities follow. You never know where opportunities will come from, so be good, do good, and watch it come back to you.

Add Value. My most successful side hustle is freelance writing. Most of my writing opportunities have come from people who found my articles on Google or read my blog, not from the dozens of applications and proposals that I've sent out. I do my best to contribute value in every facet of my life—online, among friends, and in professional settings. When people see that I have a level of expertise to offer, I automatically become a resource, which often leads to a job opportunity.

Talk About It. I was offered a job as a department administrator two weeks after telling my friends that my unemployment benefits were about to run out. I wasn't asking for a job specifically (although that's not a bad idea as you'll see in my next point), but instead I was talking openly about what I was experiencing in my life and the opportunity presented itself.

Ask. I've gotten side hustle opportunities from my Facebook statuses—no joke! Don't be afraid to take a chance and simply ask for what's available. You never know what you might find.

Utilize Social Media. Speaking of Facebook, make sure that all of your social media profiles are up to date and job search ready. It's not just LinkedIn that can help (or harm) you in a job search. You want your online persona to showcase the best of who you are, both personally and professionally. People like to know that you're not just competent in the office, but a pleasant and interesting person in general. In other words, if you have a tendency to pour your negativity into your tweets, consider finding another outlet.

Deliver. For goodness sake, when you get an income producing opportunity, work hard and put in the effort. Be prompt and professional, no matter how casual the setting. If you over deliver, you're practically guaranteed a future job opportunity.

Be Prepared for Anything. Limiting yourself to an idea of what you think you're capable of or qualified for is just that, limiting. While you should be prepared to showcase your experience and expertise in an up-to-date resume, know that general competence is applicable across many professions. If you can exhibit traits like critical thinking, ambition, and problem solving, you'll be able to more than make up for perceived gaps in experience.

Don't limit yourself to just getting by. Breaking free of broke is about maximizing your earning potential to go from surviving to thriving. While you should employ cost cutting strategies to reduce your make or break number, finding ways to increase your income beyond that minimum level is far more liberating. The more distance that you create between yourself and your make or break number, the more freedom you will have to spend your time and money in ways that serve your greater goals.

CHAPTER 13

———•·•———

Staying Motivated

Now that you know the strategies for spending consciously, eliminating debt, and growing your money, the key to success will be staying motivated through the endless ups and downs that life is bound to throw at you. In a world of social pressures, small salaries, and endless temptations to spend, it won't always be easy.

How I Learned to Follow Through

In November 2013, I ran my first marathon through the five boroughs of New York City. Those few hours were some of the most challenging and magical of my life. And while the aches and pains are now a distant memory, the lessons that I learned have stayed with me and changed my approach to every seemingly insurmountable challenge that I encounter—both financial and otherwise.

Lesson 1: Pacing Yourself Is Key

I was a gymnast growing up—high power, low endurance. I could give you 110 percent for about 45 seconds (the length of my floor routine) before collapsing with exhaustion. This made running any kind of long distance nearly impossible for me. In fact, the first time I ran a 5k, I had to walk most of it. I didn't understand how people could run more than ten minutes at a time. I decided running wasn't for me and I quit.

After graduating college and realizing that I couldn't afford a gym membership, I gave running a reluctant second chance. Maybe it was the wisdom imparted from my shiny new degree or just the fact that I was out of shape and slow, but I started to find my rhythm. With my newfound endurance, I sustained my pace through two miles, then three, and so on.

I've come to find that pacing is something that people often fail to apply outside of the track or gym, myself included. When we set new goals, we attack them with frenzied fervor, then burn out in a matter of days—110 percent can only last for so long.

After learning to pace myself for 26.2 miles, I began to apply a similar strategy to my other goals. I broke each one down into actionable steps. For instance, I set the goal of learning to write code in a single year. My first step was to find a resource. Once I found that, my next step was to use it two times per week. (I worked on coding more often, but I didn't want to set myself up for failure by saying that I would do it every day.) It's the principle of pacing in action—one small step at a time, at a sustainable rate. A month later I mastered the basics of programming and continued to move forward at my slow but effective pace.

Lesson 2: There Is Power in Commitment

When I finally ran my first half marathon, I threw up at the finish line. Yep, right in front of the cameras and cheering crowds. The thought of running the full 26.2 miles seemed as insurmountable as ever. But a year later I wound up winning the NYC Marathon lottery, and my date was set. Up until that moment, it still seemed unattainable. But as soon as I had a date, a deadline for my goal, it wasn't a matter of *if* any more, it was only a matter of *how* I would make it happen.

Having a specific target creates a remarkable sense of clarity. Suddenly, your goal isn't some distant, intangible thing, but it's a reality. With that in mind, for every step that you identified as part of your "pacing," you now have to set a time frame. This will bring about a sense of urgency and the distinct intention to achieve your goal.

Lesson 3: Stay Present

The hours I spent running the NYC Marathon were the only time in my life that I felt completely present and in the moment. To think about the race in its entirety was too overwhelming, especially around the 16-mile mark. There was so much ground left to cover, and to think of it in terms of *ten more miles* would have been too much to bear. The only way I could continue was to focus on the step that I was taking—that one breath, one moment, and nothing more.

I often find myself racing towards a finish line—the end of the work day, the end of a workout, the end of a task—rather than reveling in everything that the present has to offer. Similarly, now that you've defined your action steps and set respective deadlines, there's nothing left to do but execute your plan, one step at a time. Don't try to anticipate what's coming next. Instead, stay wholeheartedly committed to mastering the moment.

Lesson 4: Hills Suck

The NYC Marathon has a surprising amount of hills, but the one that really got me sat right at the 23-mile mark. It was *very* long and *very* slow. Even looking back now, I don't know if there was anything positive about those twenty minutes spent climbing that hill, other than the fact that it didn't last any longer.

I think that it's important to admit that some challenges and obstacles *just plain suck.* But luckily, no hill lasts forever. There's always a peak, and if you push through, you'll get there. Don't give up just because it's hard.

Lesson 5: You're Only Racing Yourself

Distance running is one of the few things in life where, unless you're an elite runner, you're only competing against yourself. Very few people compete in a marathon because they want to win; instead, they run to achieve something for *themselves.*

I find that too often I measure my success, or rather, my failures, by the success of other people. I get distracted with jealousy rather than focusing on the goals and the journey that I've so carefully crafted for myself.

I decided to take what I learned from the NYC Marathon and put it into practice. Rather than be threatened by those around me, I'm uplifted by them. They are my community and my support—we're in it together. Success isn't limited. We can all finish the race as we choose, because we're really only competing against ourselves.

So how do you translate these abstract lessons into concrete financial goals? Follow these steps…

Step 1: Start with a list.

Take inventory of your financial wants and needs by creating a list of goals. There's no judgment. This list is only for you, so allow yourself to indulge in any dream, no matter how seemingly big, impossible, or crazy it may seem. Here are some ideas to get you started:

- I want to pay off my credit card debt.
- I want to have a 6-month emergency fund.
- I want to save enough money to afford a fun and fabulous retirement.
- I want to go back to school.
- I want to buy better health insurance.
- I want to see more live entertainment.
- I want to buy new clothes.
- I want to take a dance class.
- I want to take a vacation.
- I want to buy a new computer.
- I want to buy a house.

The list can be as long or as short as you want. It should be updated as often as your needs and desires change.

Step 2: Break down your list.

For the goals that you listed, specify a realistic date, cost, and next step for each. It will take time and research to set reasonable expectations for each goal, but get started today.

Let's assume that one of your goals is, "I want to pay off my credit card debt." This is a common goal with the broke and beautiful, so let's carefully work through it together.

For the purposes of creating a reasonable debt repayment timeline, a present value calculation will be needed. Fortunately, a free debt repayment calculator like the one provided at Dinkytown.net can help us quickly and easily determine by what amount we'll need to increase our monthly credit card payments to eventually be debt free. Using the free online calculator, we input the following information:

- Current balance: $6,000
- Credit card interest rate: 14.5%
- Pay off goal: 18 months
- Current monthly payment: $200
- Additional monthly charges: $0
- Annual fee: $0

Based on these assumptions, we find that we need to increase our credit card payment from $200 to $373 per month. Next, we comb through our budget to see where we can free up cash for the additional expenditure. If not enough resources can be pooled together, we consider increasing our side hustle.

Once you get through your entire list of goals—breaking down dates, costs, and next steps for each—you may be overwhelmed. Which brings us to step 3.

Step 3: Prioritize your list.

If you did your homework in Step 2, then you should have an estimate of how much it will cost each month to achieve each of your goals. You'll likely find that you don't have nearly enough money to achieve all of your goals at once, so you'll have to prioritize. The vacation and new clothes may have to wait while you take care of your health insurance and emergency fund. Here are two options for prioritizing:

- Option 1: Rank each item on your list in terms of importance.
- Option 2: Divide your list into categories and rank each item within each category.

I prefer Option 2, since it's not realistic to put off buying new clothes until you've accomplished *everything* of higher priority on your list. By grouping your goals into categories—for example, career, leisure, education, financial security, etc.—you can create a greater sense of balance by tackling the number one priorities in each category and then working your way down each list.

Step 4: Commit!

Here comes the hard part. Breaking a habit (like smoking) or implementing a lifestyle change (like a diet) is very difficult to do, and financial changes are no different. Therefore you need to create accountability with yourself and others. Share your goals, create a support system, or use an online accountability system like Stickk.com. Don't let your dreams stay dreams forever. Turn them into tangible goals and actionable steps today.

Money Motivators

If you ever find yourself losing sight of your goals or veering off course, think about your *money motivators*. These are the reasons that you set your financial goals in the first place. Personally, I've found that my desire to build wealth is not only attached to my desire to have more of what I love, but also, a wish to have freedom from the things that I dislike.

The Most Powerful Money Motivator Is You

You've got to have a dream. Not just a career dream like being an astronaut or a movie star, but a dream of a full and intentional life, something to work towards. If you're not guided by a clear sense of purpose, you're likely to fritter away your time, energy, and money obtaining short-term achievements rather than what's really important to you.

So what is it that you're working towards? There has to be something motivating you more than, "I need to pay my credit card bill," "I need to make rent," or "I need to get my car fixed." Sure, those things are necessary, but those reasons will only make you work and save *just enough*. If you want *big* financial success, start by having a *big* dream and a clearly defined "why."

Use all five senses to experience your *why*. Right now I see the ocean and palm trees, I feel the sand between my toes, I hear the waves crashing on the shore, I taste the salty air, and I smell the warm ocean breeze. Yes, in reality I'm sitting in the economy section of an airplane, having my seatback kicked repeatedly by a screaming child, but this meditation of my dream lifestyle is what has me on my laptop, *writing*, rather than plugging into another in-flight movie. The more tangible your dream is, the more you're reminded of it, and the more you will seek to achieve it.

Getting Over Your Fear of Failure

Our dreams and fears shape our behavior, and the emotions associated with them directly influence our relationship with money. In order to master our money, we must face our fears and set goals to achieve our dreams.

Go ahead and make a list of all your fears. Not spiders and snakes, but fears related to money. For instance, "I fear credit card debt," or "I fear not having enough money to cover my expenses." Then, just as you did with your financial goals, identify the actionable steps that you can take to overcome those fears.

- I fear credit card debt so I will cut up my credit cards.
- I fear credit card debt so I will pay cash for all of my purchases.
- I fear not having enough money to cover my expenses so I will analyze my spending and see where I can cut back.
- I fear not having enough money to cover my expenses so I will find additional sources of income.

By planning ahead while you're in a logical, rational frame of mind, you'll reprogram yourself to feel confident managing your money rather than allowing an emotion like fear to control you. Allow your newfound cash confidence to pervade your life. Remind yourself of your goals by writing them down and keeping a visual reminder of them in your wallet, next to your money. Each time you open your wallet, your goals will be staring you in the face, reminding you to ask yourself "Is this purchase going to serve my long-term goals?" and "Is this bringing me closer to my *why?*"

By setting goals and changing the course of negative spending patterns, emotional spending born out of a fear of failure becomes conscious spending—and conscious spending is the key to mastering personal finance.

The secret to success is being willing to fail rather than being afraid to fail.

Develop the discipline to confront your fear of failure on a daily basis. Make it a habit to stand up to your doubts and reservations and not let them get in the way of your success. The only real failure is failing to try.

"More than education, more than experience, more than training, a person's level of resilience will determine who succeeds and who fails." – Dean Becker, President and CEO of Adaptiv Learning Systems

Stop Waiting, Start Living

Perhaps the biggest, and arguably the most important lesson that I've learned as an adult is that the rest of the world doesn't operate on a timeline based on *my* expectations—regardless of how much I wish this were true.

Rather than be frustrated by this, I've learned to turn my focus inward to the things that I *can* control. Rather than creating a timeline for results that can only be achieved when factors and circumstances outside my control come into alignment, I created a timeline for my goals that I have complete power over—like running a marathon.

Sure, I still secretly hope that my dreams of the bright lights of Broadway and subsequent buckets of money raining down on me will come true (clearly I'm not afraid to dream big), but I'm also staying grounded in my reality and working to create my own opportunities until those lucky stars align.

Constructive habits consistently applied, like tracking my spending every day, seeking new income opportunities, and finding ways to grow my money, give me ample freedom to pursue my *real* dreams.

One final confession... I love my life. I'm not wealthy or financially free—yet, but thanks to the journey I've been on the past few years, I've discovered richness far beyond anything I once thought possible. And it's only the beginning.

You now have the basics—the spending strategies, savings tactics, and money mindset. Now make it personal by picking and choosing what works for *you* and *your* dreams. Live it up and enjoy the journey!

APPENDIX

Blank Worksheets

1. Net Worth Summary

Assets	Value		Liabilities	Value
Cash/Checking			Business Loans	
Emergency Fund			Credit Cards	
Investments			Mortgage	
Personal Property			Personal Loans	
Real Estate			Student Loans	
Vehicles			Vehicle Loans	
Other			Other	

Assets $_____ – Liabilities $_____

= Net Worth $_____

2. Goals

	Short-Term 1-5 Years	Mid-Term 6-10 Years	Long-Term 10+ Years	Rank
Career				
Celebrations				
Education				
Emergency Fund				
Entertainment				
Family				
Gifts				
Possessions				
Real Estate				
Retirement				
Travel				
Vehicles				
Other				

3. Cash Flow Management

Income	Amount		Expense	Amount

Income $_____ – Expenses $_____

= Profit (Loss) $_____

4. Debt Management

Lender	Balance	Term of Loan	Interest Rate	Monthly Payment	Rank

ACKNOWLEDGEMENTS

Excerpts from this book originally appeared in Stefanie's posts for the following websites:

- Bad Credit: badcredit.org
- DebtBlag: debtblag.com
- Frugaling: frugaling.org
- Gen FKD: genfkd.com
- Prairie Eco Thrifter: prairieecothrifter.com
- See Debt Run: seedebtrun.com
- The Broke and Beautiful Life: thebrokeandbeautifullife.com
- The Well Kept Wallet: wellkeptwallet.com
- U.S. News & World Report: money.usnews.com
- VOSA: vosa.com

ABOUT THE AUTHOR

Getting by in New York from the quintessential "broke girl" perspective, NYC actress and writer, Stefanie O'Connell, lives by making her budget stretch. She chronicles her journey to find the balance between starving artist and prosperous city living on her blog, *The Broke and Beautiful Life.*

A graduate of New York University's drama and psychology programs at the height of the financial crisis, Stefanie discovered the world of financial planning out of necessity. Since then, she's been living her dream of performing while pinching pennies to make the rest of her goals a reality.

Stefanie and her work have been featured on such major media platforms as *The Wall Street Journal, USA Today, U.S. News & World Report, Forbes, Yahoo! Finance, MSN Money, AOL's Daily Finance,* and many more. Connect with Stefanie and all things Broke and Beautiful on twitter @brokeandbeau.

INDEX